IMAGES
of America

NASHVILLE
BROADCASTING

D1523478

· JOHN H. DE WITT, JR. ·
A senior student of the Duncan
Prepartory School, who designed
and installed the 100-watt broad-
castting station WCBQ of the First
Baptist church, which goes 'on the
air today with its first formal program.

Jack DeWitt was a 16-year-old student at Duncan Preparatory School when he built Nashville's
first radio station, WDAA, at Ward-Belmont School in 1922. Although radio receiving sets
could be purchased in Nashville (see the advertisement), listeners before 1922 had to pick up
stations from New York, Pittsburgh, and elsewhere. (Metro Nashville Public Library and the
Nashville *Tennessean*.)

ON THE COVER: WSM has always been proud of having a high-profile staff of professional
announcers. In the early 1960s, this group of all-stars handled the chores of delivering the news,
weather, and sports, as well as hosting talk shows and the early morning *Waking Crew* program.
They are, from left to right, Teddy Bart at the piano, Larry Munson, Bill Williams, Ott Devine,
and David Cobb. (Grand Ole Opry archives.)

IMAGES
of America

NASHVILLE
BROADCASTING

Lee Dorman

ARCADIA
PUBLISHING

Published by Arcadia Publishing
Charleston SC, Chicago IL, Portsmouth NH, San Francisco CA

Printed in the United States of America

Library of Congress Catalog Card Number: 2008937173

For all general information contact Arcadia Publishing at:
Telephone 843-853-2070
Fax 843-853-0044
E-mail sales@arcadiapublishing.com
For customer service and orders:
Toll-Free 1-888-313-2665

Visit us on the Internet at www.arcadiapublishing.com

Dedication

His WLAC listeners in the early 1960s knew him as "Big Hugh Baby." Hugh Jarrett, an original member of the Jordanaires, had a broadcast career spanning nearly 50 years at stations in Nashville, Los Angeles, and Atlanta. He was seriously injured in an automobile accident in the spring of 2008, and died following a heart attack a few months later. This book is dedicated to him. (Author's personal collection.)

CONTENTS

FOREWORD

Once upon a time in America, most radio stations—and later television channels—were locally owned and operated.

Nashville's radio stations were unique among their sister radio stations across America, because most of the singers, musicians, and engineers who made Nashville "Music City USA" and invented the "Nashville Sound" got their start in radio.

Contrasted with today's out-of-town, group-owned, ratings-ruled broadcast universe, this book depicts a time when programs and performers were rated solely by the savvy and instinct of their local employers. These folks had a vested interest in the well-being of their community. To them, broadcasting was a passion and a service rather than another profit center in a detached corporate conglomerate.

I was privileged to be a part of this era. I caught it at the tail end of its existence. And I was part of the transition to the broadcast universe of today as well. They are as different as night and day.

The comparison of the broadcasting culture depicted in this book to that of today is much akin to that of professional baseball then and now. Like the ball players back in the day, most of us got into "the business" because we weren't happy doing anything else. We did whatever it took to make the roster. We didn't make much money and we worked long hours, weekends, whenever.

And we did whatever we were assigned to do. For example, Ralph Emery covered elections as well as interviewing country music stars. Larry Munson was a disc jockey as well as a sportscaster. And Jud Collins was an Opry announcer as well as a newscaster.

Nashville Broadcasting, by veteran broadcaster Lee Dorman, is a flashback to those glory days. From an on-air personality to management and ownership, Lee has been involved in all aspects of broadcasting. Lee fell in love with "the business" when he was a kid. This book is his tribute to many of his childhood heroes and to a time remembered.

Now sit back, relax, and enjoy the show.

—Teddy Bart

Teddy Bart is a veteran radio and television news anchor, talk show host, commentator, author, and songwriter.

ACKNOWLEDGMENTS

Many people helped make this book possible in many different ways. Some contributed their ideas, some their memories, some their personal photographs, some their advice and counsel. This project, a dream and a goal for more than 30 years, would never have gotten off the ground without them. So thanks to Hudson Alexander, Nick Archer, Dennis and Vida Ball, Teddy Bart, Bob Bell, Nick and Pat Boone, Tom Bryant, Maggie Bullwinkel, Hoyt Carter, Chris Clark, Belinda Coffee, Brenda Colladay, Hudley Crockett, Larry Daughtrey, Lyle Dean, Jim DeMarco, Al Devine, Michelle Dube, John Dunning, John Fears, Claude Felton, Sam Hale, Craig Havighurst, Hope Hines, Bill Hudson, Van Irwin Jr., Rudy Kalis, Demetria Kalodimos, Evelyn Keller, Lee Kraft, Les Leverett, Terrell Metheny, Dan Miller, members of the Nash_radio Yahoo! Group, Pat Nolan, Cobb Oxford, Teri Remke, Buddy Sadler, Charlie Scott, Scott Shelton, Steve Sparks, Julia Stone, Mike Todd, Al Voecks, Bart Walker, and John Young. And most of all, thanks to my wife, Faye. She is more than a partner, she is the inspiration that drives me to reach a little higher and never ever give up.

INTRODUCTION

The story of Nashville's radio and television stations has never been fully told. In 2008, Craig Havighurst traced the history of WSM in *Air Castle of the South: WSM*. In 1989, Wes Smith's *The Pied Pipers of Rock 'n' Roll* included a chapter on the air personalities of WLAC as they related to the popularity of rhythm and blues music in the 1950s and 1960s. Now Wes is at work on a book devoted entirely to WLAC and its nighttime disc jockeys.

In the early 1970s, as a graduate student at Austin Peay, I wrote the thesis for my master's degree on the origin and growth of radio broadcasting in Nashville and Middle Tennessee. I always thought I would eventually expand it into a book that both broadcasters and listeners would enjoy reading, but it remained nothing more than a dream for the next 30 years, as career and family always seemed to push it to the proverbial back burner.

In the spring of 2008, I was in the local history section of Davis-Kidd bookstore when I came across an Arcadia book in the Images of America series on Birmingham broadcasting. Ten minutes later, I bought it, thinking how much fun it would be if I could do the same thing for Nashville. The next day, I contacted Arcadia and told them about my idea; two weeks later, I had a contract for this book.

I started in radio by building my own small station (it covered about a six-block area around my home) when I was 16. My first paying radio job was at WDBL in Springfield, Tennessee, just weeks after I graduated from high school. I worked at stations in Clarksville and Nashville all through college, and after graduating, I was hired as news director at WKFR in Battle Creek, Michigan. From there I went to WILX-TV in Lansing, where I anchored the 6:00 and 11:00 p.m. news for nearly two years before deciding to return to Austin Peay and graduate school. My old station in Clarksville, WDXN, needed a program director, and Austin Peay had a graduate assistantship available, so I was in business. Between 1974 and 1991, I went from programming to sales to sales management to station management with ownership interest in Clarksville, Waukegan, Milwaukee, and Nashville. Finally, in the mid-1990s, I did what so many people with a background similar to mine do—I became a consultant.

While writing this book is the fulfillment of a dream, it is only one of several that highlight my broadcast career. Others were being hired at the age of 19 as a disc jockey at WKDA, then Nashville's number-one radio station; being hired at just 23 to anchor the 6:00 and 11:00 television news in Lansing, Michigan; and finally, being named general manager of WLAC radio in 1982. This was Nashville's second radio station, with a long, proud history that I had written about in my thesis. And at the age of 38, here I was, running it. What a great feeling.

Now I am excited about the opportunity to bring you the story of all of Nashville's original radio and television stations—those that went on the air between 1922 and 1970. Here are the people you grew up listening to on the radio and watching on television. You will see them as they looked in front of the cameras, behind the microphones, and relaxing in their leisure time. I sincerely hope you enjoy this trip down memory lane.

One

NASHVILLE RADIO
THE EARLY YEARS

Nashville's broadcasting history began in May 1922, when 16-year old John "Jack" DeWitt Jr. installed a 20-watt transmitter at Ward-Belmont School. WDAA was born because Dr. C. E. Crosland, associate president of Ward-Belmont, saw the potential advertising value of a radio station to the school. WDAA broadcast sporadically for nearly a year before the college decided it could not afford to continue financing its operation.

In November 1922, 150-watt WOAN in Lawrenceburg sold its old transmitter to a group of Nashville businessmen, who would found WDAD in 1925. But before that happened, there would be one more serious attempt to start a new station as well as two amateur "club stations" (WABV in 1923 and WEBX in 1924).

The one serious attempt was WCBQ by the First Baptist Church. It operated at 1270 on the dial, and its call letters stood for a church slogan referring to the congregation's approach to its services: "We Can't Be Quiet." W. A. Marks, a member of the Business Men's Sunday school class and owner of an auto repair shop, contributed more than $1,500 to the project, and on March 18, 1924, a test program was broadcast. On Sunday, April 6, WCBQ made its official debut.

Two years later, ownership of the station was transferred to a partnership of two successful Nashville businesses, Braid Electric Company and Waldrum Drugs. WBAW (for Braid And Waldrum) set up studios in the Capitol Theatre in downtown Nashville. The financial terms of the sale included a payment to the church of $1 and an agreement to broadcast all of its services free. In 1929, the station was sold to Col. Luke Lea, publisher of the Nashville *Tennessean*, and the call letters were changed to WTNT (for The Nashville *Tennessean*). The station lasted less than a year because of Colonel Lea's financial problems.

Nashville's second station of note was WDAD, which first took to the air in September 1925 (one month before WSM). It was owned by Dad's Auto Accessories and broadcast on 1330. Dad's owner, Lovell Smith, started the station thinking it would help him sell automobile and radio accessories.

In October 1925, WSM was begun by the National Life and Accident Insurance Company. WLAC followed the next year, and the rest, as they say, is history.

Many of the nation's earliest radio stations were started by churches looking for ways to take their message into the homes of people who were too old, too ill, or just unable to get to their services. Nashville's First Baptist Church gave the city WCBQ, its second radio station, in 1924. (Metro Nashville Library and the Nashville *Tennessean*.)

Dr. W. F. Powell, pastor of the First Baptist church, is seen in the above photograph delivering an address in his pulpit. The address is being made into the radio microphone.

Dr. W. F. Powell, pastor of Nashville's First Baptist Church, has the distinction of delivering the first local radio address in Nashville—his sermon, on Sunday, April 6, 1924. (Metro Nashville Public Library and the Nashville *Tennessean*.)

While still in his teens, Jack DeWitt helped build several of Nashville's first radio stations, and he was not yet 20 when WSM debuted in October 1925. (Grand Ole Opry archives.)

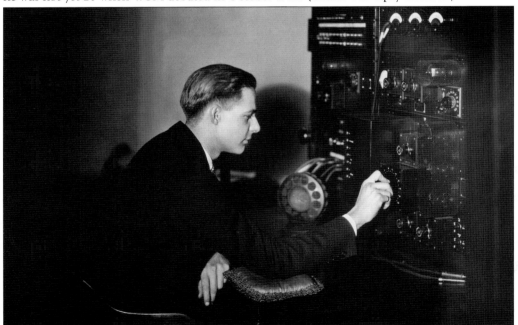

Thomas Parkes was WSM's first chief engineer. His top assistant was young Jack DeWitt. Edwin Craig and the National Life and Accident Insurance Company provided the station with the most modern equipment available. (Grand Ole Opry archives.)

WSM has employed many well-known announcers over the years. Some gained national prominence, while others became Nashville institutions. One of the earliest to man the WSM microphone was Albert "Tiny" Stowe, so named because he weighed 250 pounds. (Grand Ole Opry archives.)

Another of WSM's early announcers was Ott Devine. He was with the station for over 40 years, eventually becoming program director and Grand Ole Opry manager. (Al Devine.)

National Life created WSM as an extension of its insurance company, believing rural Southerners would be more receptive to their sales agents (called "Shield Men") if they first heard about them on the radio. This early advertisement from a National Life newsletter was meant to bring the company closer to the station's listeners. (Grand Ole Opry archives.)

WSM announcers Tiny Stowe and Jack Baker welcome Johnny Roventini, the Phillip Morris bellhop, to Nashville. He became famous on radio, and later television, for his cry, "Call for Phillip Mor-r-r-iss." (Grand Ole Opry archives.)

One of WSM's most popular programs in the late 1920s and early 1930s was Sunday Down South. Broadcast live from the spacious auditorium in the original National Life building in downtown Nashville, it featured "music in the Southern manner" and was sponsored by the Lion Oil Company. (Grand Ole Opry archives.)

This postcard shows the small hut erected behind the WSM transmitter building and tower in Brentwood, just off Concord Road. Every day when the renowned *Pan American* passenger train would pass by, the station would broadcast the sound of the engine's whistle as it first approached and then faded into the distance. (Author's personal collection.)

Here is the WSM crew on the *Pan American* doing a remote broadcast, including Jack DeWitt (fourth from the left), engineer Aaron Shelton (kneeling) and announcer Harry Stone (far right). (Grand Ole Opry archives.)

Announcer Ott Devine (left) and engineer Aaron Shelton (right) take part in an early WSM remote broadcast as they transmit from Mule Day festivities in Columbia, Tennessee, in the 1930s. (Al Devine.)

On another WSM 1930s on-location broadcast, this announcer describes the action at a golf tournament at Richland Country Club. (Grand Ole Opry archives.)

Jack Keefe, one of WSM's first announcers, was also a singer and entertainer; a graduate of Harvard University and Vanderbilt Law School; and a chemist and professor of bacteriology at Vanderbilt Medical School. Keefe became WSM's first sports announcer when he did the play-by-play broadcast of Vanderbilt football games in 1926. (Metro Nashville Public Library.)

WSM sent listeners this postcard to acknowledge their having received the station. In radio's early days, stations could be heard hundreds of miles away, and listeners often collected cards like this. Avid radio fans would see who could pick up a station farthest from where they lived. (UV201. com and Mike Schultz.)

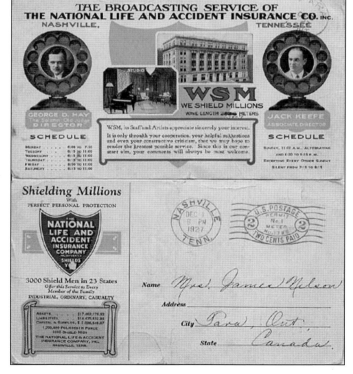

WLAC offered listeners this official certificate when they wrote to the station describing where they had listened and what they had heard. (UV201.com and Mike Schultz.)

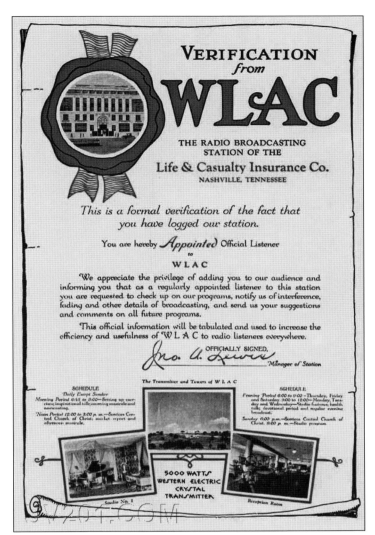

WLAC, started by Life and Casualty Insurance Company in much the same way National Life had created WSM, printed these tickets to publicize the station and the insurance company. Known as the "South's Master Station," WLAC adopted the slogan "Health, Thrift, Entertainment, and Education." (Author's personal collection.)

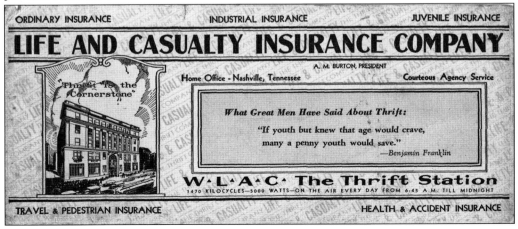

In radio's early years, broadcast engineers were always looking for ways to improve their station's coverage. In addition to transmitter power and antenna height, ground conductivity and terrain played a big role in how far away a station's signal could be heard. WSM employed a field test car in which the station's engineers would drive around the area and test the station's signal strength. (WSM Radio.)

WSIX first went on the air in Springfield, not Nashville, on January 7, 1927. Jack and Louis Draughon, who operated the 638 Tire Service, set the station up in this building at Sixth Avenue and Locust Street in downtown Springfield. The station's call letters, WSIX, reflected the six in 638 Tire Company. (Author's personal collection.)

Two

RADIO'S BIG THREE
WSM, WLAC, WSIX

The radio stations acknowledged as Nashville's "Big Three" all went on the air in the 1920s—WSM in 1925, WLAC in 1926, and WSIX in 1927. WSIX actually began not in Nashville, but in Springfield, when Louis and Jack Draughon, owners of a service station known as the 638 Tire Service, traded five barrels of oil for a 100-watt transmitter. In 1936, they decided to move the station to Nashville, setting up studios in the Andrew Jackson Hotel.

WSM, meanwhile, had increased its power and moved to 650 on the dial, its present position, and was solidifying its position as Nashville's preeminent station, in part because of the popularity of the *Grand Ole Opry* and the NBC radio network. WLAC, a CBS affiliate, had moved from 1470 to 1510 on the dial, increased its power, and enjoyed success with network shows like *Myrt and Marge*, *Stoopnagle and Bud*, and Fred Allen's *Bath Club Revue*, as well as local music and information programs, coverage of news events, and traffic reports from downtown Nashville.

As the 1930s gave way to the 1940s and World War II, news reports took on more importance. Jud Collins, Ernie Keller, and Ott Devine at WSM; Tim Sanders and Herman Grizzard at WLAC; and Jack Wolever and Jim Kent at WSIX brought the news to Nashvillians in the days before one could simply turn on a television and quickly catch up on the day's events. At night, all three presented extended newscasts much like those now watched at 6:00 and 10:00 p.m. on television.

The programs on Nashville's three radio stations (there would be no new stations until the late 1940s) varied. WSM featured country, classical, and popular music, including the Piano Twins, Francis Craig and his Orchestra, Beasley Smith and his Orchestra, Dinah Shore, and Phil Harris. At WLAC, some of those same bands, plus *The Ole Dirt Dobber* program (which was sent out nationally on the CBS network), were favorites. At WSIX, many local singers as well as the highly popular ABC network show *Don McNeill's Breakfast Club* topped the programming schedules.

As 1950 approached, Nashville listeners had an ample choice of programs and entertainment from which to choose.

WSM's Jud Collins was the [illegible] on the scene during the Tennessee Maneuvers in 1941-42.

Jud Collins was lured to WSM from WSGN in Birmingham in 1940 by station manager Harry Stone. In 1941, he went into the field to cover army maneuvers near Manchester, Tennessee, during the early days of World War II. (Grand Ole Opry archives.)

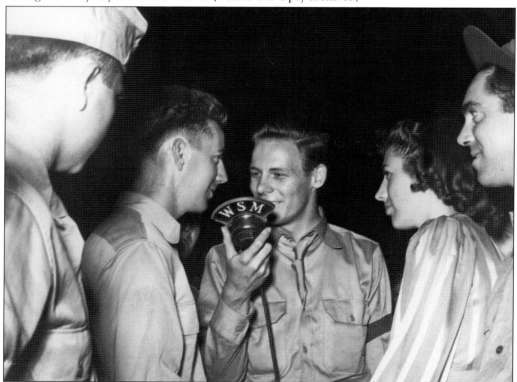

Later in the summer, taking WSM microphones, engineers, and photographers, Jud (center) interviewed Tennessee soldiers in the field at army maneuvers in Louisiana. The station hoped listeners would appreciate WSM bringing them news about their sons. (Grand Ole Opry archives.)

During World War II, new car production came to a halt while automobile manufacturers produced war machinery. In 1946, cars began rolling off the assembly line for the first time in five years. Here Nashville mayor Thomas L. Cummings (left) and Tom Springfield (right), manager of the Nashville Automobile Club, are interviewed by a WLAC newsman (holding the microphone). (Metro Nashville Public Library.)

In 1945, WLAC broadcast Gov. Jim Nance McCord's swearing in and inaugural address from the War Memorial Auditorium in downtown Nashville. (Metro Nashville Public Library.)

WSM has always had Nashville's largest announcing staff. In this photograph, which accentuates the beautiful art deco furnishings and WSM studio design of the 1940s, are, from left to right, David Cobb, Tom Stewart, David Stone, Jack Harris, Ott Devine, and Harry Stone. The Stones were brothers, and Harry would become WSM's station manager. (Grand Ole Opry archives.)

WSM announcer Louie Buck (holding the microphone) reports from a Wendell Willkie for President rally at the Nashville airport in 1940. The man standing to Buck's left, wearing the light-colored hat, is Jack Stapp, another WSM staffer who later resigned to manage WKDA. (Grand Ole Opry archives.)

WSM's "air family" in the 1940s included, from the top left, David Cobb, Grant Turner, Ernie Keller, Ralph Christian, Louie Buck, Lionel Dican, Jud Collins, Irving Waugh, and Ott Devine. Waugh would go on to become president of WSM in 1968. (Grand Ole Opry archives.)

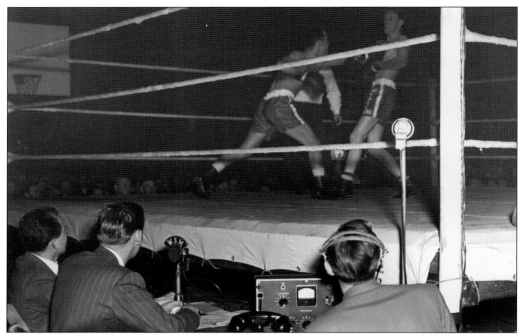

Ott Devine (left) and Jud Collins (center) give listeners the blow-by-blow description of a Golden Gloves match at the Hippodrome on West End Avenue. (Grand Ole Opry archives.)

Dr. IQ was an NBC network program which aired nationally from 1939 until 1950. In his book *On The Air*, radio historian and novelist John Dunning describes the show as "the first great quiz show of the air." Featuring quizmaster Lew Valentine, the show would occasionally go on the road, as it did in this photograph when the program was broadcast live from Nashville on WSM. (Grand Ole Opry archives.)

Announcer Ernie Keller performed many functions at WSM radio and television over the years. Here he boards a U.S. Air Force cargo plane to report back to Nashville from military maneuvers in Alaska. (Evelyn Keller.)

Just back from serving in the navy during World War II, Nashville native and Vanderbilt graduate Van Irwin Jr. started WNAH on Christmas day, 1949. Shown on its first day of broadcasting, Irwin, now 89, still runs the station, which holds the distinction of being Nashville's oldest broadcast facility operated by its original owner. The station began with studios in the James Robertson Hotel and later moved to the Hermitage Hotel but now is in its own building on Music Row. (WNAH radio.)

Ken Bramming was one of Nashville's most versatile and durable broadcasters. Barely out of his teens when he became an announcer at WSIX in the late 1940s, Ken was still on the air at WAMB in the 1990s. (WKRN television.)

In 1941, WSM, which had pioneered AM radio in Nashville, gave America its first FM station, known as W47NV. It lasted for 10 years, then went off the air. (Grand Ole Opry archives.)

Three

NASHVILLE GETS NEW RADIO STATIONS

During the 20-year period between 1927 and 1947, the only new station to go on the air was WSM's experimental FM in 1941, which broadcast classical music on a noncommercial basis. It went off the air in 1951 when WSM president Jack DeWitt decided to put the station's emphasis on television, seeing greater potential growth and revenue. Because so few people had FM radios in the 1940s, the station never had any impact on the market.

In 1947, Nashville got its fourth radio station. WKDA went on the air in January, owned by Thomas Baker, sales manager for 11 years at WLAC, and Alvin Beaman, who owned the local Seven-Up bottling company (and later Pepsi) and Beaman Pontiac. The station's 340-foot tower was located atop Rutledge Hill on Second Avenue South at Peabody Street.

Legendary sports announcer Larry Munson was WKDA's first sports director. He told local radio fan and historian Hudson Alexander the story of his famous 1954 on-air blooper and resulting suspension, which has become a local urban legend in Nashville:

> Hell, I was doing a baseball game between the Nashville Vols and New Orleans. I thought I had switched back to the station, but back at the studio, they had left my microphone open. I turned to one of the guys in the booth there at the ballpark and I say . . . "ain't this a helluva way to make a G-- D--- living!" Now, just as you might expect, that didn't go over too well with the management people, and I was suspended from the air pretty fast after that little deal.

But listeners loved Munson, and when they demanded that the station put him back on the air, it did.

During the next few years, WNAH, WMAK, and WSOK (now WVOL) became Nashville's fifth, sixth, and seventh stations. WNAH featured religious programs and gospel music; WMAK played popular adult music; and WSOK set out to become a station that would, in the words of original owner Cal Young, "be devoted exclusively to a Negro listening audience and employing all Negro personnel." True to his word and his vision, the station has always been an asset to Nashville's black community.

WSM still had Nashville's largest staff of announcers in the 1950s. They were, from left to right, (first row) David Cobb, Louie Buck, Ott Devine, and Tom Hanserd; (second row) Dave Overton and Grant Turner; (third row) Dick Shively, Jud Collins, Ernie Keller, and Ralph Christian. Shively did the sports at the station before the arrival of Larry Munson. (Grand Ole Opry archives.)

The *Waking Crew* was a long-running and highly popular early morning program on WSM radio and television that began in 1950. Shown here are the studio orchestra and singers, and in the foreground are host Dave Overton (left, with bow tie) and weatherman Bill Williams (facing Overton). (Grand Ole Opry archives.)

WGNS in Murfreesboro has been an important part of that community ("GNS" stands for "Good Neighbor Station") since it first went on the air in 1947. During the Korean War, Johnny Long and other area bands performed for the troops at nearby Sewart Air Force Base, and WGNS broadcast the programs over the Liberty Radio Network. (Bart Walker.)

WSM farm director John McDonald, who hosted the popular *Noontime Neighbors* program, mans the station's booth at the Tennessee State Fair as Jud Collins (arms crossed) relaxes in the background. (Grand Ole Opry archives.)

In the 1950s, WSIX was playing "middle-of-the-road" music—soft pop hits—and Ken Bramming's smooth, rich, voice introduced the songs to listeners. (WKRN television.)

Jim Kent started at WSIX in 1942 at the age of 18 and remained with the station for 42 years. Between 1955 and 1975, he became involved in community theater and had leading roles in more than 30 productions. (WKRN television.)

WSM has had its share of well-known, highly respected, and much-loved announcers over the years. One of the best was Grant Turner, who had worked at stations in Texas and Knoxville before coming to WSM in 1944. A longtime country music deejay and Opry announcer, Turner died in 1991. (Les Leverett collection.)

While its format was gospel and religious programming, WNAH ventured into secular broadcasts with the play-by-play of Lipscomb College baseball games in the 1950s. The station also featured Chicago White Sox baseball and Notre Dame football games and was Nashville's Mutual Network affiliate for several years. (WNAH radio.)

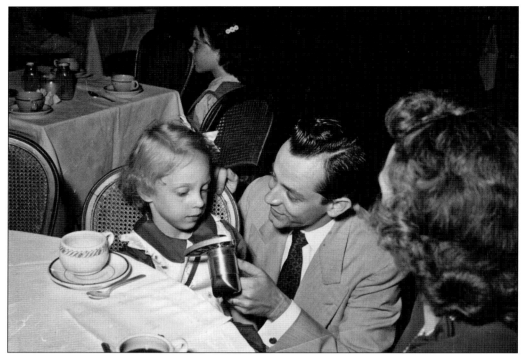

In the early and mid-1950s, WMAK was playing popular adult music, having not yet made the switch to rock and roll. One well-received program was *Luncheon at the Noel*, aired live at noon each weekday from the dining room of the Noel Hotel. (Author's personal collection.)

WSM has always had the largest news department of any Nashville radio station. Here Houston Roberts works on a developing story that involves sound bites on tape. (Grand Ole Opry archives.)

Noel Ball (seated), who was arguably Nashville's most popular disc jockey during the 1950s, began his career as a teenage announcer in Norfolk, Nebraska, where he had been a schoolmate of Johnny Carson. (Vida Ball.)

Audie Ashworth was one of WKDA's top-rated announcers. Working from 7:00 p.m. until midnight in the late 1950s and early 1960s, Audie left radio to go into the music business and was replaced by the equally popular Bill Berlin. (Bonnie Ashworth and jjcale.com.)

Sam Hale grew up in McMinnville, Tennessee, starting in radio there in 1954. After two years in the army, he came to WKDA in 1959 and quickly became one of the station's most popular personalities. (Sam Hale.)

Here Sam oversees a contest winner receiving her grand prize—a telephone call to a singer with a hit record. After leaving Nashville, Sam worked at stations in Milwaukee and later Atlanta, where he still resides. After a very successful radio career, he left broadcasting and went into the financial field. (Sam Hale.)

Terrell Metheny became a highly popular WKDA deejay in the late 1950s using the air name "Ronn Terrell." After just a couple of years he moved on to larger markets, including Milwaukee (WOKY) and New York (WMCA), and became one of the nation's top radio programmers. (Terrell Metheny.)

WKDA
RONN TERRELL FAN CLUB

THIS IS TO CERTIFY THAT . . .

_____
(member's signature)

IS A MEMBER OF THE RONN TERRELL FAN CLUB, AND IS ENTITLED TO ALL BENEFITS, INSULTS, AND INDIGNITIES RONN CAN SCHEME UP.

THE HOLDER OF THIS CARD IS ALSO GIVEN A MEMBERSHIP IN THE "SAPM" (SOCIETY FOR THE ADVANCEMENT OF POPULAR MUSIC).

Keep this card for valuable prizes

Terrell built a loyal audience of young listeners as WKDA grew in popularity and became Nashville's top-rated station. His fan club was one of the first in Nashville for any radio personality. Terrell has retired and now lives in Arkansas. (Terrell Metheny.)

As a teenager in Nashville, Pat Boone and a young singer named Joyce Paul had a Saturday morning program on WSIX called *Youth On Parade*. Although he lived in east Nashville, many residents of west Nashville remember Pat's Saturday afternoon appearances at the Belle Meade Theater's Happiness Club (Brenda Lee was another regular guest). In 1955, he began his rise to national stardom with "Ain't It A Shame." (Pat Boone.)

While a student at David Lipscomb College, Pat also made regular appearances on WLAC. After transferring to Columbia University, Pat's career took off. He appeared in the 1957 movie *April Love* and continued to have hit records and star in movies throughout the 1960s. (Pat Boone.)

Four

THE ROCK AND ROLL RADIO WARS

As it moved through the 1950s, Nashville now had seven radio stations. Four had network affiliations: WSM (NBC), WLAC (CBS), WSIX (ABC), and WNAH (Mutual); the other three were independents. While the network stations had the luxury of airing local programs and filling the rest of the time with network shows, the independents were responsible for filling all of their airtime locally. For this reason, recorded music began to take over the airwaves—there just was not enough local talent to fill the hours of available time or money to pay performers what it would cost. As a result, WKDA, WMAK, and WSOK/WVOL began playing records and were known as "music stations." WNAH broadcast church-related programs, ministers' spiritual messages and talks, and gospel music. When Cal Young started WENO, it became Nashville's first full-time country music station.

The late 1950s saw the beginning of the famous "radio wars" between WKDA and WMAK. The two were always competing for the top spot in Nashville's radio ratings (which determined who got the best advertising buys and therefore made the most money), trying to outdo each other in every way. If one station had a contest with a $5,000 prize, the other tried to give away $10,000. Jingle packages were big, too. Former WKDA announcer and now ad agency owner Bill Hudson enjoys telling how WMAK paid thousand of dollars for a new jingle package, but before they could get it on the air, WKDA manager Jack Stapp had Roger Miller (then a writer for Stapp's Tree publishing company) duplicate it in the studio. The minute it was done, Stapp put it on WKDA. Tricked and embarrassed, WMAK never aired the package they had paid dearly for.

Fifty years later, listeners still remember when deejay Ken Knight, in a publicity stunt being pulled by stations across the country, locked himself in the WMAK control room. Demanding a raise, he announced he would not leave the studio until he got it. He then played the same song, "Your Ma Said You Cried in Your Sleep Last Night" by Kenny Dino, for 24 hours in a row.

Despite leaving more than 40 years ago, Larry Munson remains one of Nashville's favorite broadcasters. Working at WKDA and WSIX before moving over to WSM in the late 1950s, he was the play-by-play voice of both the minor league baseball Nashville Vols and the SEC's Vanderbilt Commodores following Dick Shively. (Les Leverett collection.)

T. Tommy Cutrer was WSM's most popular country music deejay of the late 1950s and early 1960s. He not only had a nightly show on the station but was also a featured announcer on the Grand Ole Opry. (Les Leverett collection.)

Bill Williams read the news and did general announcing at WSM but was best known as "the Rhyming Weatherman" on the morning *Waking Crew* program. Coworkers say Williams would ad lib the weather forecast from wire copy, making up the rhymes as he went along. As Channel 4's weatherman, he replaced Dr. Carl Seyfert, a Vanderbilt astronomer who was killed in an automobile accident in 1960. (Les Leverett collection.)

As WSM's farm director and host of *Noontime Neighbors*, John McDonald's popularity among listeners in rural areas was enormous, as evidenced by the mail he received every day. (Les Leverett collection.)

In the 1950s, a listener could tune in almost any radio station in Nashville and hear commercials for Frosty Morn bacon and sausage. Kids and adults would be at school or work, singing about how it was every little pig's dream that "he would be good enough to be a Frosty Morn." The packing company headquartered in nearby Clarksville was one of Nashville's biggest advertisers on radio and television for more than two decades. (Rainbo Records and Baltz Brothers/Elm Hill Meats.)

Playing the top chart songs as well as introducing records for new artists who would visit him at the station each night, Ralph Emery often had to chomp down a sandwich between records. Prior to being hired at WSM, Ralph, who was from McEwen, Tennessee, worked briefly at WNAH and WSIX and studied broadcasting under WLAC's John Richbourg. (Demetria Kalodimos.)

In addition to being a popular radio deejay and television host, Noel Ball (on ladder) was also in the music business, producing the 1958 hit "Oh, Julie" for the Crescendos. In his spare time, he was a licensed pilot and loved to fly. (Vida Ball.)

Noel Ball, like many other Nashville radio personalities of the era, made numerous personal appearances to promote his program and his station. This advertisement was to drum up business for the Hickory Q restaurant in west Nashville after Ball had moved from WMAK to WSIX. Many radio listeners remember Noel's favorite catch phrase as he returned from a commercial break: "This is the Ball . . . we bounce." (Metro Nashville archives and Vida Ball.)

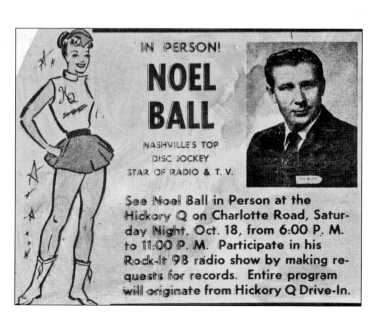

IN PERSON!

NOEL BALL

NASHVILLE'S TOP DISC JOCKEY STAR OF RADIO & T. V.

See Noel Ball in Person at the Hickory Q on Charlotte Road, Saturday Night, Oct. 18, from 6:00 P. M. to 11:00 P. M. Participate in his Rock-It 98 radio show by making requests for records. Entire program will originate from Hickory Q Drive-In.

One of WLAC's leading nighttime personalities was John Richbourg, known to his listeners as "John R." Sponsored by Ernie's Record Mart, John sounded black on the air and never did anything to dispel that notion. If anything, he encouraged it with his style, delivery, and choice of music. When not on the air at WLAC, he taught radio at the Tennessee School of Broadcasting. His students included Hudley Crockett, Ralph Emery, and John Lashlee, all of whom became top Nashville broadcasters. (Jim Lowe.)

The cast of characters that made up WLAC's night air staff is legendary. While the station during the day was quite conservative, after 7:00 p.m., everything changed when the rhythm and blues jocks took over. They were, from left to right, John Richbourg, Gene Nobles, Bill "Hoss" Allen, and Herman Grizzard. In the background is newsman Don Whitehead. Radio insiders always found it ironic that while many listeners thought the white disc jockeys were black, the only WLAC announcer who really was black was Whitehead. Another member of the crew was Hugh Jarrett, who replaced Gene Nobles in the early 1960s while Nobles battled crippling arthritis. Jarrett also hosted the weekly Hugh Baby Hop dances at the National Guard Armory. (Jim Lowe.)

A young Gene Nobles was gaining popularity and notoriety playing rhythm and blues music at night on WLAC. Nobles, born in Hot Springs, Arkansas, in 1913, was a former carnival barker, bingo dealer, and announcer on several small Southern radio stations before coming to WLAC in 1943. For years, his program was sponsored by Randy's Record Shop in Gallatin, owned by Randy Woods, who went on to found Dot Records. (Metro Nashville Public Library.)

Colorful Language Makes Nobles Top As Disc Jockey

When radio listeners spin their dials to a disc-jockey and hear such outlandish phrases as "latch onto," "jerks," and "little fillies," instead of the customary drollery of the boys who ride the nation's turntables, said radio audience is inclined to check its hearing aids and lean closer to catch more of the provocative language.

Such is the case when dynamic Gene Nobles, emcee of the Sterling (Beer) Dance Hour, The Midnight Special, and Record Highlights, demonstrates his waxed disc over Station WLAC in Nashville, Tennessee.

Station WLAC is impressed by Gene's amazing rise as the favorite platter spinner of Nashville's discriminating radio audience. But Gene's sponsors, Buckley Amusement Co. and Randy Record Shop, declared that they had received a very impressive amount of letters for orders for records.

Nobles set Nashville agog last year with his verbal antics. His colorful "Slamguage" has touched up the sarcastic vocabularies of the nation's younger set, which is Gene's chief stock in trade.

Gene Nobles, emcee of Sterling's Dance Hour, Midnight Special, and Record Highlights, first became a part of radio when he joined Station WABO as a junior announcer at $17.50 per week. . . . Later joined WLAC. . . . First break came when he emceed record show called Sterling Dance Hour. . . Then Gene convinced Station WLAC that there were a lot of listeners after twelve o'clock so he sold the Midnight Special. From then on it has been a series of successes for Gene Nobles, disc-jockey of WLAC.

In 1962, WMAK was still trailing WKDA in the ratings as the two powerhouse rock stations fought it out for listeners. But they had a great lineup of air talent, including Allen Dennis, making the first of his many appearances over the years at Nashville radio stations. (Nick Archer.)

Bill Hudson worked at WKDA in 1962 and was considered one of the best commercial production people in radio. He left the station and at 23 started his own advertising agency. For 45 years, Bill Hudson and Associates has counted some of the city's most prestigious businesses among its clients and has won numerous awards. (Bill Hudson.)

Roger Schutt, better known to Nashville radio listeners in the 1960s and 1970s as "Captain Midnight," was one of WKDA's most unique personalities. Always working the all-night shift, Schutt would appear and disappear, be fired and rehired, and always be described by even those who knew him best as "one strange dude." (Nick Archer.)

Khan Hamon, who now lives in Texas, worked at WKDA in the mid-1960s using the air name "Charlie Brown." He is best remembered for his attempt to break the world record for continuous broadcasting without sleep during a station promotion from the Preston Lincoln-Mercury showrooms in 1964. (Khan Hamon.)

Disc Jockey Dreams On— Fame Secure Despite Halt

Charlie Brown, the Nashville radio disc jockey who drifted to dreamland on a hospital-bound stretcher at 4:26 p.m. Friday after staying awake and on the air for more than 124 hours, awoke at 2 a.m yesterday.

An hour later, Charlie went back to sleep.

Since 3 a.m., according to nurses at St. Thomas Hospital, Charlie has been snoozing intermittenttly—waking up and looking around and then drifting back into what has been called "that somnabbulistic state of glorious, oblivious glee."

THE NURSES SAID they have no idea when Charlie will leave St. Thomas, where he was taken on doctor's orders after making a very respectable bid to break the world's disc jockey stay-awake record

He is listed in fair condition. His doctor ordered him to go to sleep—over Charlie's determination to go on—after it became apparent the exhausted disc jockey was suffering from tonsilitis, a leg inflamation and a high fever.

None of his ailments were brought on by his sleepless vigil, the physician said, but he added that all were aggravated by it.

Charlie's fame as a WKDA announcer is secure, though, despite his forced surrender to the arms of Morpseus before the battle was won. His horde of teen-aged followers are convinced he will make it yet — and that he could have this time had not illness interfered.

WHEN HE finally gave up and got on the hospital stretcher Friday, Charlie's words were a little woozy and

capable of a couple of days more, at least. But then came the illnesses.

He had been staying awake by taking as many as three showers at a time, shaving, and then coming back to the mike and the telephone to talk to the hordes of young well-wishers.

Now, of course, it's all history—unless Charlie decides to try it again.

WKDA often promoted concerts featuring artists whose records the station played. Here the "Good Guys," including, from left to right, Bill Berlin, Captain Midnight, Bill Craig, "DJ Dan" Hoffman, Dick Buckley, and Doc Holliday, welcome the Shangri-Las, who had a hit with "The Leader of the Pack." (Nick Archer.)

Here are the WKDA Good Guys in 1966. From left to right are Captain Midnight, Doc Holliday (noon–4:00 p.m.), program director Dick Buckley (9:00 a.m.–noon), "DJ Dan" Hoffman (6:00–9:00 a.m.), Bill Berlin (8:00–midnight), and Bill Craig (4:00–8:00 p.m.). (Nick Archer.)

In the 1960s, the radio wars between WKDA and WMAK were legendary. Each station tried to top the other in its choice of music, number of records played per hour, customized PAMS station jingles (listeners would often request their favorite jingle instead of a song, like "W-K-D-A—1240—home of the 'Good Guys' ") and contests and prizes. The author was a WKDA Good Guy at this time, having replaced Captain Midnight in 1964, and is the bottommost deejay in the image at right. (Author's personal collection.)

While WKDA was number one in the ratings for 12 years in a row from the mid-1950s through most of the 1960s, WMAK was usually number two. On this survey are their top personalities, including Gene Clark (who later founded Spotland Studios in Nashville) and longtime Nashville radio favorite Allen Dennis, who worked in Nashville at least four different times over a 30-year period. (Author's personal collection.)

Oh, Where Have the 'Good Guys' Gone?

Gary Edwards
Circus animal trainer

Dave Allen
With Shelby Singleton

Dick Buckley
To locate here

Roger Schutt
With Robert Holladay Co.

Doc Holiday
In Murfreesboro

By PAT SWINGLEY

THEY wore sweatshirts instead of white hats and they finished first instead of last because they were the Good Guys to Nashville's youth.

WKDA was one of the first stations in the country to promote the image, beginning in 1959, and through the years there were some 35 disc jockeys to bear the insignia.

They donned their Good Guy sweatshirts and appeared at record hops and shows, played in basketball games and participated in school activities.

Bill Craig
On West Coast

Dan Hoffman
Peoria program director

J. Thomas
In Jacksonville

Don Bowman
Country comedian

This newspaper article in the Nashville *Tennessean* chronicled where some of the WKDA Good Guys had gone. Note the inclusion of J. Thomas, now a well-known stand-up comedian (as Jay Thomas) and star of television and movies. (Metro Nashville archives.)

Radio stations have always looked for ways to promote themselves with exciting contests, great prizes, and anything that will get publicity. WMAK put out this album of popular oldies in the mid-1960s. On the cover at the bottom left is Gene Clark, and at the bottom right is Allen Dennis. (Author's personal collection.)

Allen Dennis was one of WMAK's most popular air personalities, working at the station several different times as a solo act beginning in the early 1960s and later with Alan Nelson and then Darrell Douglas as part of a two-man show. A Chattanooga native, Allen also worked for stations in that city and in Birmingham. He returned to Nashville in the 1980s and worked at WSM. (Author's personal collection.)

Cal Young started two Nashville radio stations—WSOK (now WVOL), which he later sold, and WENO, licensed to Madison and for many years Nashville's only full-time country music station. Young believed in high-profile promotions, like this one for Gates Tires. (Metro Nashville archives.)

Buddy Sadler, a Nashville native and Middle Tennessee State University student in 1964, broke into radio that year doing commercials for Plaza (bowling) Lanes on WKDA with the author. He went to work at WLAC-FM in 1965, later working at WHIN in Gallatin then WKDA and WSM as a newsman. (Buddy Sadler.)

Despite earning its top spot in the ratings with music and popular deejays, WKDA also had an aggressive news staff. Here program director Dick Buckley (standing) is shown with news director Gary Edwards, who had received a tip from a disgruntled former assistant to New Orleans district attorney Jim Garrison critical of his much-publicized investigation of the Kennedy assassination. (Nick Archer.)

WSIX newsman Charlie Scott (left) is shown here interviewing Rick Jason, costar of the 1960s ABC television series *Combat*. Scott was a newsman at WLAC before moving over to WSIX, where he worked for more than 30 years. He still does occasional voice-over work in Nashville. (WKRN television.)

Bill Allen (left) was involved in WLAC's news operation before he became "the Hossman," a popular nighttime air personality at the station. He is shown here with WLAC's news director, Roland Wolfe. Allen, a graduate of Vanderbilt University, also was active in the music business, owning the Hermitage Records label for many years. (Metro Nashville archives.)

In the mid- and late 1960s, WSIX tried playing popular music and going head-to-head with WKDA and WMAK. Air personalities (from top left to bottom right) were Buzz Benson, Bob Bell, Noel Ball, Ed Sheppard, and Chuck Caldwell. The experiment did not work, and the station changed its format to metropolitan country shortly thereafter. (WKRN television.)

Many radio and television stations use outdoor advertising to promote themselves, particularly during ratings periods. Here is a WSIX radio billboard calling attention to the station's news department. (WKRN television.)

Nashville's first new AM station in a number of years went on the air in 1962 when Nashville optometrist Dr. Sam Simon and a group of friends started WLVN (Lovin' Country). When that format did not work, the station became WWGM (Wonderful World of Great Music) and claims longtime WSM announcer Tom Bryant and WGN Chicago newsman Lyle Dean as alumni. Shown here are station manager Darrell McMurray (left) and Nashville Symphony director Willis Page (right). (Metro Nashville archives.)

WNFO went on the air in 1963 with studios in the 1808 West End Building. Shown here is owner Ira Trotter (standing) with Charlie Richardson, one of the station's announcers. After only a couple of years of independent operation, the station was sold and became WKDA-FM and later WKDF. (Metro Nashville archives.)

Webber Parrish, WLWM president, tunes up equipment for his new FM station.

Nashville businessman Weber Parrish started WLWM-FM in 1962, moving into studios off Charlotte Pike on Thirty-seventh Avenue North. In 1968, he sold the station, and it became the second WSM-FM. (Metro Nashville archives.)

WLAC's Skyway Patrol gets you where you're going. Easier. And faster.

During the peak traffic hours, morning and afternoon, we give you the sky line on traffic.

Our flying officer broadcasts traffic conditions as they happen. He tells

you where the congestion is, and where it is not. Which means you can avoid snarls and stalls. You save time. And temper.

It's the only way to drive.

Listen. 1510.

In recent years, many radio stations have provided their listeners with air traffic reports during morning and afternoon drive time. But the first station to offer the service, in 1966, was WLAC, with its *Skyway Patrol* helicopter reports. (*Nashville!* magazine and Metro Nashville Public Library.)

Two of Nashville's top radio personalities of the 1950s and 1960s ended up working together at the same station. Ken Bramming (left) and Noel Ball (right) both hosted radio and television programs at WSIX. (WKRN television.)

Fred Goree hosted a show on WVOL in 1966. The station has always captured a huge segment of Nashville's black listenership, but in recent years, it has had to share that audience with WQQK-FM, 92Q, which appeals to the area's growing black youth with its rap and hip-hop music. (Metro Nashville archives and the *Tennessean*.)

CHUCK "CHAZZ THE GLAD DAD"
MITCHELL
News Director
Mon.-Fri. 8:00 P.M.-Midnight

"SIR EDWARD PAUL" HALL
Production Chief
Mon.-Fri. 12:00-2:00 P.M.
and 5:00-7:00 P.M.

NOW . . . AT LAST
WVOL YOUR GOODWILL STATION is on FULL TIME!

After many months of careful preparations your Goodwill Station, WVOL, is prepared to serve this Community on a FULL TIME BASIS!

Beginning Friday, January 29, 1960, WVOL will sign on the air at 5:00 A.M. and STAY on the air until midnight . . . offering you fine entertainment . . . news . . . sports events . . . and spiritual uplifting.

Here you see the people who will have the responsibility of serving you NINETEEN HOURS EVERY DAY!

MORGAN "HAPPY JACK" BABB
Program Director
Mon.-Sat. 6:00-9:30 A.M.

LOUISE FLETCHER
Woman's Director
Mon.-Sat. 9:30-10:00 A.M.
and Mon.-Fri. 2:00-3:00 P.M.

REV. W. E. JASPER
Religious Director
Mon.-Sat. 5:00-6:00 A.M.
and 10:00-12:00 Noon

CLARENCE "MR. TUNE"
KILCREASE
Mon.-Fri. 3:00-5:00 P.M.
Sat. 8:00 P.M.-Midnight

ED BLACKMAN
Account Executive

NOBLE BLACKWELL
Account Executive

DEACON CHARLES ARNOLD
Special Events Director
Mon.-Fri. 7:00-8:00 P.M.
Sun. 6:00 P.M.-Midnight

SISTER LUCILLE BARBEE
Sun. 10:00-11:00 A.M.

HOWARD "MR. RHYTHM" CLARK
Sat. 5:00-7:00 P.M.

BOOKER T. AKINS
Building Superintendent

WAYNE B. ROBINSON
Chief Engineer

AUGUSTUS "GUS" MITCHELL
Engineer

GEORGE LITCHFIELD
Engineer

MARIAN J. SIMPSON
Continuity Director

ROBBIE GREENE
Traffic Director

ROBBYE DAVIS
Accountant

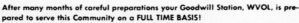

WVOL

GOODWILL • ENTERTAINMENT • COMMUNITY SERVICE
5000 Watts • 1470 On Your Dial

CARTER S. JONES
Manager

WILLIAM D. SALMON
Assistant Manager

WVOL, despite several changes of ownership, has always dedicated itself to Nashville's African American community. Dr. Morgan Babb, Clarence Kilcrease, Chuck "Chazz" Mitchell, Howard Clark, Noble Blackwell, and a teenage Oprah Winfrey have worked at the station over the years. (Sam Hale.)

Five

THE RISE OF FM RADIO

The 1970s were an exciting time in Nashville's radio history. The biggest development was the growth of FM. In the late 1950s, Bill Barry and Bill Baird started WFMB, playing what some called "elevator music" and what later would be a very popular format called "beautiful music" (played in Nashville on WZEZ). WFMB would become WLAC-FM, later becoming WKQB in the late 1970s, WJYN in the early 1980s, and WLAC-FM again in the mid-1980s.

WSM bought WLWM-FM in 1968 and changed the call letters to WSM-FM; and the station became very popular in the mid- and late 1970s as SM95. WNFO-FM, started in 1963, was purchased by WKDA and became WKDA-FM and later WKDF. Playing the hardest rock music of any station in Nashville, it went on to become known simply as KDF, developing a cult-like following larger than that of any other station in Nashville's history.

This was also the time when stations in bedroom communities like Lebanon, Gallatin, Murfreesboro, and Hendersonville began to increase their power, update and upgrade their programming, and attempt to become "Nashville" stations, thus reaching larger audiences and increasing their opportunity to sell more advertising and make more money. WBYQ-FM (92Q) in Hendersonville was the first to do this, followed by WKYX-FM (Kicks 104) in Gallatin; WYHY-FM (formerly WCOR) in Lebanon; and WZKS-FM (96 Kiss) in Murfreesboro. Later WWTN, licensed originally to Manchester as WMSR-FM and owned by singer Wayne Newton's brother before he lost it because of what the government called his "shady dealings," moved its tower and transmitter to Williamson County.

Because of the success of these stations and FM's superior sound quality, AM stations began switching to other types of programming, including news and talk. Of the original AM stations in Nashville, only WSM (country music), WLAC (news and talk), WVOL, and WNAH remain. WKDA, WMAK, WSIX, and WENO are either gone or have converted to nontraditional programming. Two later stations, WAMB (big band) and WNSR (sports) are also still on the air, and WWGM moved to Gallatin. More than two-thirds of today's radio listeners say they prefer to listen to FM.

Scott Shannon, on the air at WMAK in the early 1970s when the station was at the peak of its power, became Nashville's number-one radio personality with his nighttime program. Calling himself both "Supershan" and "your leeeader," Scott left Nashville after a couple of years, eventually ending up in New York, where he became a top-rated deejay and programming guru. He now has his own oldies network in conjunction with ABC as well as an Internet oldies station and is the voice introducing syndicated national talk show host Sean Hannity. (Nick Archer.)

There has only been a select group of radio personalities in Nashville whose career extended over a 30-year period. One of them is Coyote McCloud, who followed Scott Shannon at WMAK in the 1970s, went on to continued success at Kicks 104 and Y-107 in the 1980s and 1990s, then played the same songs he helped make popular when they became classics at Oldies 96.3 and 97.1 in the early 2000s. Having built a large and loyal following, it was only natural that a Coyote McCloud Fan Club would follow. (Teri Remke.)

1300 / WMAK

COYOTE McCLOUD

Coyote McCloud teamed up with Wendy's spokeswoman Clara Peller when she became famous for her "Where's the Beef" commercial. In 1984, Coyote wrote a song as a promotional vehicle for the Wendy's campaign and got national recognition with this album. (Coyote McCloud, A&M Records, and Wendy's International.)

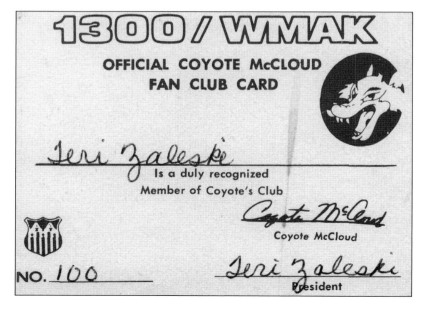

Coyote McCloud's popularity not only took him to the top of Nashville's radio ratings but also led to the creation of a fan club. Teri Zaleski was one of a number of self-described "radio groupies" who helped Coyote become one of Nashville's all-time favorite deejays. (Teri Remke.)

MARK DAMON

Another popular personality at WMAK during its high-flying days as a top-rated rock station was Mark Damon, also known as "Doc" Damon. He continued to garner high ratings after moving over to WLAC, as did the equally popular Dick Kent. (Teri Remke.)

KRIS BRADLEY

Another popular WMAK personality during their most successful years in the early and mid-1970s was Kris Bradley. (Teri Remke.)

Here is the lineup of WMAK personalities in the mid-1970s: Allen Dennis in the morning; Gary Douglas (using his real name, Gary Beaty, he later worked at WSM-FM); John Young in the early afternoon (he is now in Atlanta and does a lot of voice-over commercial work); Dick Kent in the late afternoon; Scott Shannon at night; and Rick Stuart overnight. (Nick Archer.)

Coyote McCloud is back, this time at WYHY-FM, also known as Y-107. His popularity here still placed him near the top of Nashville's radio ratings, only now he was doing mornings 6:00–10:00 instead of nights. (Nick Archer.)

Mary Glen Lassiter, a Gallatin native, first became popular at the original 92Q WBYQ-FM (in Hendersonville, an oldies station) in the late 1970s and early 1980s. She has been both a morning show personality as "Proud Mary" and a morning drive news anchor, working alone and as part of a two-person team. After moving to Atlanta for a few years, where she reunited with former 92Q morning personality Steve McCoy, she returned to Nashville and 105.9 The Rock. (Mary Glen Lassiter.)

MARY GLEN LASSITER

WLAC-FM has gone through many incarnations, playing everything from beautiful music to heavy metal. In the late 1970s, the station was known as WKQB and competed with KDF. Nick Archer, in addition to many other radio talents, made a great mascot, appearing at station functions as the "K Q Bee." Here he is pictured with actor Gary Busey and two young fans. (Nick Archer.)

Gerry House has had one of Nashville radio's longest and most successful careers, almost all of it at WSIX. He started there in 1975, and *The House Foundation*, with supporting cast members Paul Randall, Al Voecks, and Duncan Stewart, got its start in the early 1980s. It has been the number one rated program among adult radio listeners in Nashville for nearly three decades. (WSIX radio.)

The House Foundation split up in 1985 when Gerry left for WSM. He was there for one year before moving to Los Angeles and KLAC. He came back to Nashville in 1987 and returned to WSIX, where he still holds court each weekday morning from 6:00 until 10:00 with cast members Mike Bohan, Stewart, Voecks, and House-created characters like Mack Truck, Homer, and Maurice. (Les Leverett collection.)

After years as a star at what is arguably Nashville's strongest music station ever, known to its loyal fans simply as 103 KDF and playing heavy rock music, Carl P. Mayfield switched over to country music. After trying afternoons at WSIX to complement the station's strength in the morning with Gerry House and *The House Foundation*, he went back to KDF when the station switched from progressive rock to a country music format. He left there and most recently had a program on Sirius satellite radio. (Citadel Broadcasting and WKDF.)

Although it had declined in the ratings somewhat with the growing popularity of FM, WKDA-AM was still around in the late 1960s and early 1970s. The lineup here includes Don Sullivan, who went on to work later at WSIX, and J. Thomas, known today as comedian Jay Thomas. (Nick Archer.)

Readers will be meeting Pat Sajak, who graced the airwaves of WSM-TV before moving on to national popularity, in the chapters that follow on television in Nashville. He was also a top-flight radio personality, hosting an afternoon program daily on WSM-AM in the mid-1970s. (Nick Archer.)

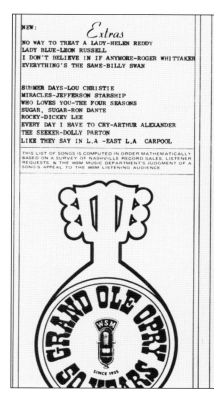

Donna Brake   Mike Donegan   Gary Beaty   Keith Bilbrey   Steve Henderson

Kris Bradley   Andy Pearson   Marijo Monette   Karen Gerson   Jim Driver

In the mid- to late 1970s, one of Nashville's highest rated radio stations was WSM-FM, also known as SM95. Playing soft rock music, these personalities made the station very successful for about five years. (Nick Archer.)

Teddy Bart took his years of experience as a talk show host at WSM and news anchor at WNGE and hosted an extremely popular talk show in the early and mid-1980s on WLAC-AM. (Teddy Bart.)

Ruth Ann Leach had been a news anchor and reporter at Channel 5 before she, too, began hosting a talk show on WLAC, along with Teddy and the third member of the news/ talk trio, Les Jameson. She also wrote a column for the now defunct *Nashville Banner*. (Ruth Ann Leach.)

Tom Bryant was a longtime announcer and production whiz at WSM after working briefly at WWGM in the early 1960s. He is now retired but still lives in Nashville. (Tom Bryant.)

A popular WSM announcer, programmer, and production person, Ted Johnson left that station and is now the owner and general manager of Nashville's first full-time sports station, SportsRadio 560 WNSR. (Ted Johnson.)

Ken Bramming is shown still plugging away behind the microphone in the 1980s, playing big band music and hosting monthly dances on WAMB. (Bart Walker.)

Jack Stapp, who had worked at WKDA in the 1930s and 1940s, left that station to become general manager of WKDA in 1957. He also was the founder of Tree Publishing, one of country music's most successful music publishing companies. (Debbie Tenpenny.)

Six

TELEVISION COMES TO NASHVILLE

Television came to Nashville in 1950. WSM, Nashville's first AM station (in 1925) and FM station (in 1941), was also the city's first television station. When Jack DeWitt and Ott Devine welcomed a hoped-for 10,000 potential viewers (that is how many television sets there were said to be here in 1950) and motioned to announcer David Cobb and singer Dottie Dillard to start their program, Nashville joined the television age. Early programs at WSM made use of the station's top radio personalities: Cobb, Dave Overton, Jud Collins, and Ernie Keller. Joining the lineup of NBC network programs were the *Noon* show, the *Five O'Clock Hop*, the *Waking Crew*, the *Channel 4 Club*, *Bozo the Clown*, and a number of country music programs featuring *Grand Ole Opry* stars.

In 1953, WSIX-TV became Nashville's second television station. As Channel 8, it featured ABC network shows plus local favorites like *Live Studio Wrestling*, *Bop Hop*, *Youth on Parade* starring a teenage Pat Boone, *Romper Room*, and *Shock Theater*. Top personalities at the station included Noel Ball, Jim Kent, Ken Bramming, Gil Greene, Jack Joyner, and Hudley Crockett.

In 1954, WLAC-TV joined Nashville's television community, affiliating with the CBS network. Because of early morning shows hosted by Eddie Hill and later Don Howser, WLAC became very strong among viewers in predominantly rural areas. Other popular local programs included *Popeye*, *Bobo the Clown* (with Bob Lobertini), *Buffalo Bill* (with Bill Jay), *Woods 'n Waters* (an outdoor show with Jay and Bill Clay), and *Slimnastics* (with Lobertini and Jackie Bell). Top personalities on WLAC included Bill Jay, Bob Lobertini, Bill Shell, Tom Mayhew, and Rick Moore. Channel 5 also featured Nashville's first female weatherperson and first black program host.

In 1963, WDCN-TV, Nashville's public television station, went on the air, operated by the Metro Board of Education on Channel 2. Top programs over the years have included *Sesame Street*, *Mr. Rogers*, and locally, *Jellybean Junction*, *A Word on Words* with John Seigenthaler Sr., and *Tennessee Crossroads*.

In 1968, Nashville's first independent television station went on the air as WMCV. It was also Nashville's first UHF station, operating on Channel 17. Today it is known as WZTV and is a Fox Network affiliate.

WSM, which had been Nashville's pioneer radio station in 1925, was also Nashville's first television station, going on the air for the first time at 1:10 p.m. on September 20, 1950. With chief engineer Aaron Shelton directing the action, WSM president Jack DeWitt (left) and announcer Ott Devine (right) welcomed viewers. At the time, there were an estimated 10,000 television sets in Nashville. (*Nashville!* magazine and Metro Nashville Public Library.)

The first live program to be telecast on WSM featured, from left to right, announcer David Cobb, model Carolyn Malone, bass player Walt Summers, singer Dottie Dillard, model Rhoda Horvath, and guitar player Harold Bradley. (Grand Ole Opry archives.)

A VISIT TO THE NOON SHOW

MINISTER OF THE WEEK

SPECIAL GUESTS

SONGS BY DELORES WATSON

Nashville's Number One TV personality, Jud Collins, serves as host of the festivities. His warm and folksy manner make "Noon" an integral part of Nashville daily living.

GARDENING TIPS

"NOON" AND JUD COLLINS ARE HOUSEHOLD WORDS IN NASHVILLE . . . FOR "NOON" IS NASHVILLE'S LIVE SESSION OF INFORMATION AND ENTERTAINMENT.

Precisely at 12:00 sharp, Poppa John Gordy and his Dixieland Band swing into a fine rendition of New Orleans style music to start off the hour-long program.

WSM-TV's News Expert Bill Williams keeps the "Noon" viewers up-to-date with a look at the news. (The format . . . it's in Bill's head!)

For the housewife, Billie Jean Dorris, a former "Mrs. America" contest runner-up, holds a kitchen corner with recipes, sewing notes, and fashion items.

In addition to anchoring the nightly news on Channel 4, Jud Collins also hosted the *Noon* show. A highly popular program for more than three decades, it featured Collins's easy style with interviews, music by the WSM orchestra and singers, homemaking and gardening tips, visits from area spiritual leaders, and special guests. Later the program was hosted by Teddy Bart. (Demetria Kalodimos.)

Jud Collins, who had been with WSM radio since 1940, was an easy choice to become Nashville television's first news anchor. His soft manner and easy approach endeared him to Nashville's early television viewers, even if the news set was somewhat primitive. Jud passed away in December 2008. (Demetria Kalodimos.)

Not long after the television station began to grow in popularity, it also grew in sophistication. The look of the news set for Jud Collins was much more visually pleasing. Collins became like a member of the family to many Nashvillians, who invited him into their homes every night at 10:00 for the news, sponsored by Fidelity Federal Savings and Loan. (Demetria Kalodimos.)

The *Five O'Clock Hop* was Nashville's version of *American Bandstand*. Each weekday afternoon, Dave Overton, who also hosted the *Waking Crew* each morning, counted down the top hits and best-selling records. (Grand Ole Opry archives.)

High school students from all across the city competed for the chance to squeeze into Channel 4's studio and dance to the most popular songs of the day. In the jargon of the day, teens thought it was really cool to get on the show. (Grand Ole Opry archives.)

Channel 4 had the *Five O'Clock Hop* with Dave Overton, so Channel 8 countered with *Bop Hop*, hosted by Jack Joyner. The concept was the same, the music was the same, and the "sock hoppers" probably were, too. Guests who made appearances on the show included Jimmy Rogers, Andy Williams, and Eddy Arnold. (WKRN television.)

THE MAGAZINE WITH FAST & SLOW LISTINGS

TV PRESS

YOUR LOCAL GUIDE TO TV
COMPLETE PROGRAM LISTINGS
Week Of Aug. 25 - 31

15¢

Noel Ball's "*Saturday Showcase*" . . . See Page 4

SATURDAY SHOWCASE

WITH NOEL BALL

Saturdays -:- 2:00 P. M.

wsix-tv Channel 8

Noel Ball, already Nashville's most popular radio personality among teens and young adults at WKDA and then WMAK, moved over to WSIX and was given a television show, *Saturday Showcase*, as part of the deal. (WKRN television.)

After having had a local show on WSIX in the early and mid-1950s, Pat Boone in 1958 had his own weekly network program on ABC. It was carried locally in Nashville on the station where it had all begun just a few years earlier. (WKRN television.)

Earlier Ken Bramming was described as one of Nashville's most versatile broadcast personalities. Here he shows why, as he appears in the guise of "Dr. Lucifur," host of Channel 8's weekly *Shock Theater.* (WKRN television.)

WSIX, like Nashville's other two television stations at the time, promoted their programs with billboards, bus signs, newspaper advertisements, and in this case, signs on the back of taxicabs. (WKRN television.)

While Bob Lobertini is probably Channel 5's best-known weatherman, Jean Hughes holds the distinction of being Nashville's first weatherwoman. She handled the chores for a short time at WLAC-TV in 1955. (Newschannel 5 Network, Nashville.)

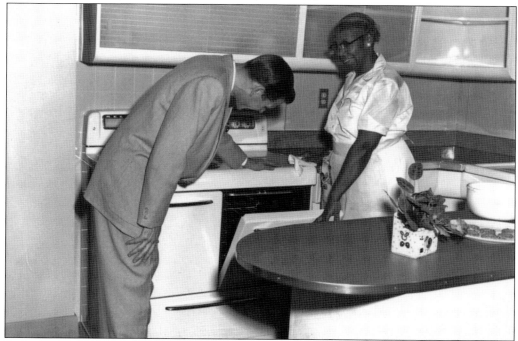

Eudora Boxley is believed to be the first African American woman to have her own television program in Nashville and one of the first in the country. She hosted *Southern Cooking with Eudora Boxley* on Channel 5 in the mid-1950s. (Newschannel 5 Network, Nashville.)

Marge Cooney (left) was one of the women pioneers in radio. Her first job at WSM was playing the piano with Beasley Smith in the 1930s on a program called *The Piano Twins*. Later, in the 1940s, she was the host of *A Woman Looks at the News*, and using the air name "Ann Ford," she also hosted a program called *The Man I Married*. When WSM-TV went on the air in 1950, she hosted an early cooking show. Here she is shown with Grace Zibart (right). Marge passed away in 2001 at the age of 95. (Grand Ole Opry archives.)

Phila Rawlings hosted another early cooking show on WSM-TV called *Kitchen Kollege*. She moved to Clarksville after she married Adolph Hach. As Phila Rawlings Hach, she became a popular caterer, continued to write cookbooks and make personal appearances, and with her husband opened a successful restaurant called Hachland Hill. (Grand Ole Opry archives.)

One of the most popular television programs of the 1950s was the nationally franchised *Romper Room*. In Nashville three women hosted the show over its 18-year run: "Miss Norma" (1955–1961), "Miss Eleanor" (1961–1964), and "Miss Nancy" (1964–1973). Here Miss Norma (seated) welcomes 14-year-old Nashville teenage singing sensation Brenda Lee. The show's first host, Norma Tate Coverdale, had been a teacher at Donelson Elementary School when she answered a newspaper advertisement and won the job over more than 100 other applicants. She left the show after six years to have a baby. (WKRN television and Brenda Lee.)

WSM-TV director Bayron Binkley was Happy A. Clown (left) and Boyce Hawkins was Grandpa Moses (right) on *Grandpa, Happy, and the Three Stooges* in the 1960s. WSM also produced *Happy Town* with Dave Overton as the Mayor and featuring Grandpa Moses and Happy A. Clown. (Les Leverett collection.)

Just as area teens longed to be in the studio audience of the *Five O'Clock Hop*, elementary school students made up the weekday afternoon "peanut gallery" of *The Channel 4 Club* in 1954. In addition to host Ernie Keller, the show featured Poindexter the Dog (and soon-to-be famous puppeteer Tom Tichenor). The author is in the audience, fourth from left in the top row. (Grand Ole Opry archives.)

Occasionally the programs went on the road. Here Ernie Keller, Poindexter the Dog, and a young girl share the stage as the show was broadcast on location from the Tennessee State Fairgrounds. Not only was Keller a host of the children's shows at Channel 4, he also filled in on the news desk, was the television spokesman for Purity Dairies, and was the public address announcer for Vanderbilt University football and basketball games. (Grand Ole Opry archives.)

Look who's back! It is Ken Bramming again, this time as host of the *Mickey Mouse Club* on Channel 8. Sponsored by Kroger and featuring local Mouseketeers, the show ran from 1954 to 1959. How Bramming got his first television job was told in the *Nashville Scene* after his death in 1997: "After the war, Bramming visited his parents, who had moved to Nashville. He planned to leave after a few weeks, but a lucky break involving one of Nashville's most famous sons made him stay. 'Pat Boone was scheduled to be on the announcing staff at WSIX,' Bramming said, 'when he got his break with Arthur Godfrey and had to go to New York. So I took his place on television. I hadn't been on TV. They put me in there, cold turkey, and said, "You'll do." ' " (WKRN television.)

Bill Jay (left) was to WLAC-TV what Jud Collins and Dave Overton were to WSM. In addition to anchoring the station's newscasts and outdoor shows, Jay was "Captain Bill," hosting *The Little Rascals*, *Cartoon Carnival*, and *Popeye* between 1958 and 1962, when he turned the helm over to "Captain Bob" (Lobertini). (Newschannel 5 Network, Nashville.)

In addition to anchoring the news, *Popeye*, *Woods 'n Waters*, and sometimes the weather and sports, Bill Jay also found time to dress up as Buffalo Bill for an afternoon kids show. (Newschannel 5 Network, Nashville.)

Another popular Channel 4 program for kids was *Ruffin Reddy*. Jim Sanders, a local actor well known in Nashville's theater circles, was the cowboy host. The show was sponsored by one of Nashville's most recognizable businesses, Pops-Rite Popcorn. (Tim Hollis.)

Ruffin Reddy aired every weekday afternoon and featured contests, prizes, and Western serial movies starring Roy Rogers, Gene Autry, Hopalong Cassidy, and all the other cowboy heroes. (Grand Ole Opry archives.)

Bob Lobertini played straight man to one of Nashville's best-known puppets of the 1950s and 1960s, Bobo the Clown. Kids on the show would shriek with laughter when given the opportunity to honk his nose. (Newschannel 5 Network, Nashville.)

Making a repeat performance is Jim Kent. He, too, made the transition to television, appearing here as Captain Crook, host of an afternoon kids show. With him is his real-life son, Beau, appearing on the show as a boy named Saturday (so as not to be confused with Robinson Crusoe's Friday). Twenty years later, Beau would himself be an announcer at WSIX radio. Jim's voice, by the way, was the first one heard on WSIX-TV in its initial broadcast. (WKRN television.)

WSIX-TV was Nashville's second television station, broadcasting for the first time at 1:00 p.m. Sunday afternoon, November 29, 1953. The first year it was an affiliate of CBS, ABC, and the now-defunct DuMont networks, but in 1954, it went full time with ABC, dropping the other two. "The Shows Are Great on Channel 8" read the advertisements and flyers, as WSIX promoted itself and its programs just after it went on the air. (WKRN television.)

Channel 8's early newscasts were anchored by Hudley Crockett, who had been hired at WSIX radio as a sportscaster when Larry Munson left to go to WSM. Crockett was a Nashville native and a graduate of West High School (class of 1951) and Austin Peay State College. After nearly 20 years in broadcasting, he was named press secretary for then-governor Buford Ellington and later ran unsuccessfully for the U.S. Senate. He is now retired but still lives in Middle Tennessee. (WKRN television and Hudley Crockett.)

Bill Jay, Channel 5's multitalented announcer, host, and newsman, anchored the news each night on *Newsbeat* on WLAC-TV. (Newschannel 5 Network, Nashville.)

In the mid-1960s, Channel 5's news anchors were Bill Williams (left) and Merle Emery (right). This was not the same Bill Williams, of course, who worked at Channel 4 and WSM radio in the 1950s and 1960s. (Newschannel 5 Network, Nashville.)

WSM/WSMV dominated the nightly news ratings for decades before Channel 5 and Chris Clark pulled even and in some periods passed Channel 4 in the fight for viewers. Before WSMV's *The Scene at Six* and *The Scene at Ten*, Channel 4's news was called *Dateline Today*. Here the anchors are, from left to right, Jud Collins, Boyce Hawkins, and Al Voecks. (Demetria Kalodimos.)

In addition to his news, announcing, and kids show responsibilities, Bill Jay also anchored the sports on Channel 5 in the late 1950s. (Newschannel 5 Network, Nashville.)

Bill Jay, (left) like his Channel 4 counterpart Larry Munson, loved fishing and the outdoors. Here he teams up with cohost and sponsor Bill Clay for the popular *Woods 'n Waters* show on Channel 5. (Newschannel 5 Network, Nashville.)

Many commercials were performed live in the early days of television. Here a young Ken Bramming is doing a commercial for a product called *Waterfoil* on WSIX. (WKRN television.)

One of Nashville's favorite television personalities in the early days of WSIX was Gil Greene, a very popular young man who hosted programs, did commercials, and could deliver the news, weather, and sports, too. Station coworkers were stunned one day when they were informed that he had taken his own life. Longtime WSIX newsman Charlie Scott says that, to this day, the suicide remains an unsolved mystery to his former coworkers. (WKRN television.)

A popular local program on Channel 8 in the late 1950s and early 1960s was *Live Studio Wrestling*, featuring local promoter Nick Gulas and sponsored in part by jeweler Harold L. Shyer ("If you don't know diamonds, know your jeweler . . . and if Harold says it's so, it's so"). Well-known local wrestlers included the fabulous Fargo Brothers, the Greenes, the Von Brauners and their dapper manager "Gentleman" Saul Weingeroff, and Tojo Yamamoto. (WKRN television.)

WSIX took advantage of the opportunity to be seen by thousands of viewers with this booth and display at the Tennessee State Fair. (WKRN television.)

WDCN-TV held numerous fund-raising events, being a public television station, the largest of which was the *Action Auction*. An early event was this 1960s fashion show featuring a number of prominent Nashville women. (WNPT and WKRN television.)

1 FADE IN:
Beverly Mathis, modeling a Moonglo beret, mans a
spare camera for a three-shot of Mrs. George Cate in
a ranch mink cloche; Mrs. Tom Turbeville, a darker
ranch profile; and Mrs. Charles Howell, III, wearing
snow mink with jeweled bandeau. The mink touch is
from Chayburke's, Sixth Avenue.

Just as all Nashville auto dealerships made a splashy show of new car introductions every September, television stations did the same thing with the fall lineup of network programs. WSIX-TV rented the Tennessee Theater, often referred to as "the showplace of the South" for its ornate design and furnishings, and invited the city's leading business owners, advertisers, and ad agencies to a preview of the 1957 television season. Notice the easel board with the photograph of James Garner starring in *Maverick*, one of ABC's top-rated shows, and the movie poster for *Escapade In Japan*, starring Theresa Wright and Cameron Mitchell. (WKRN television.)

Bob Johnstone had sung with Paul Whiteman in New York on the *Philco Hall of Fame* radio show in the late 1940s as well as with the orchestras of Shep Fields and Nashville's Owen Bradley and Beasley Smith before coming to WSM. He was the first featured vocalist on the *Waking Crew* and *Noon* shows. After leaving the station, he began a second career as a commercial artist, and from 1970 to 1990, he was the vice president and artistic director for the National Poster Company in Chattanooga. He retired back to Nashville in 1990 and died in 1994. (Grand Ole Opry archives.)

Buddy Hall was WSM's second featured vocalist, coming between Bob Johnstone and Teddy Bart. According to Craig Havighurst in *Air Castle of the South: WSM*, Hall, a former Arthur Godfrey *Talent Scout* singer, was one of 38 vocalists who auditioned for the job at WSM when Snooky Lanson left Nashville to join the cast of the network program *Your Hit Parade*. (Les Leverett collection.)

WSM used this visual display to convince advertisers of the station's ability to sell groceries for H. G. Hill, Kroger, and Cooper and Martin stores in Middle Tennessee in the 1960s. (Demetria Kalodimos.)

WSM-TV had been on the air for seven years, using an antenna at its studio site at Fifteenth and Compton Avenues near Belmont College, when it decided to construct a new tower. Choosing a location near Thirty-seventh Avenue North in west Nashville, the antenna—at the time the tallest in the country—was nearly completed in 1957 when guy wires apparently snapped and the tower collapsed, sending three construction workers to their deaths and crushing this truck in the process. The antenna site was then moved to Knob Road, where a new tower was built adjoining the land where the station's new studios were later constructed in 1966. (Grand Ole Opry archives.)

Seven

THE BIG THREE
GET BIGGER

Television in Nashville came of age in the 1960s and 1970s. In the early years, television in Nashville was much like television elsewhere—primitive, crawling, and learning how to walk. The sets for news, weather, and sports were sparse and often unattractive. The personalities who anchored the programs were usually radio people who had been recruited to television because there were no seasoned television veterans—the medium was still too new.

But as television grew up, stage sets became more visually pleasing, the equipment more sophisticated, and the talent more experienced. One example is the weather set. Early weather boards utilized black markers and small wooden or plastic clouds and suns with magnets glued on the back. Sometimes they did not work as planned, and a high-pressure front over Minnesota would slowly slip toward the Gulf of Mexico because a magnet had lost its magnetism. Such events often provided early television personalities with some harrowing moments (Channel 8's Ken Bramming said it happened to him and got him fired). New weather equipment such as Doppler radar and the increased use of trained meteorologists as weathermen made reporting and predicting the weather at least appear to be more accurate.

The increasing use of special reporters in the fields of health and fitness, personal finance, and politics broadened the scope of local newscasts, and investigative reporting by Larry Brinton, Phil Williams, and Nancy Amons, among others, pepped up the local newscasts. And who will ever forget Huell Howser's *Happy Features* on Channel 4?

Pat Sajak and Oprah Winfrey both passed through Nashville on their way to fame and glory—Pat at WSM radio and television and Oprah at WVOL and Channel 5. Also bringing a measure of distinction to Nashville was *Hee Haw*, a top-rated program across the country produced at Channel 5. Chris Clark, Dan Miller, Teddy Bart, Al Voecks, Bob Bell, Larry Munson, John Lashlee, Barbara Moore, Ralph Emery, Eddie Hill, Bobby Lord, and Porter Waggoner are only some of the names that come to mind when one thinks of television in Nashville in the 1960s and 1970s.

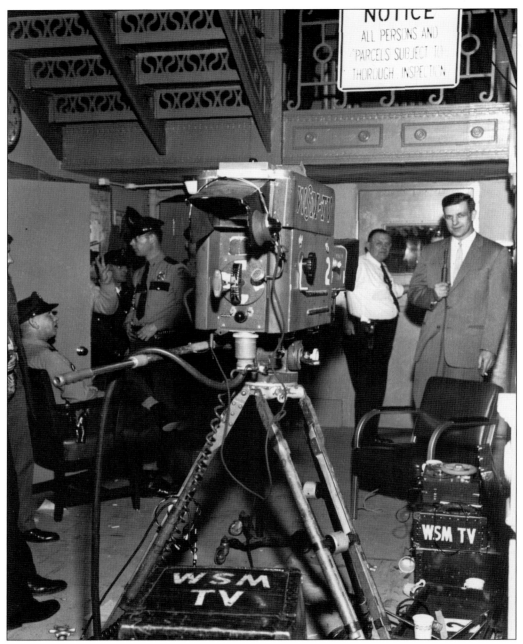

In April 1960, a group of prisoners took guards hostage at the Tennessee State Penitentiary. WSM immediately sent a television crew to the prison on Centennial Boulevard in west Nashville to cover the uprising. Ralph Christian reported on the events until the crisis was peacefully settled. (Les Leverett collection.)

The coverage of the uprising and hostage crisis was what station officials described as a "team effort." Jud Collins, Ralph Christian, audio and video engineers, and production crew members worked in front of and behind the cameras and microphones to bring the drama into Nashville's homes. Note the man in the top photograph (with binoculars) wearing a holster and handgun. (Grand Ole Opry archives.)

Bill Williams (left) and Jud Collins (right) had an easy manner and smooth rapport when they worked together on the *Noon* show on Channel 4. (Demetria Kalodimos.)

Al Voecks, who was first and foremost a newsman for much of his career, also doubled as a weatherman from time to time on WSM-TV. Voecks came to Nashville from Iowa and has been on the air here for more than 40 years, first at WSM and now at WSIX-FM, where he delivers the news on *The House Foundation* show weekday mornings. (Al Voecks.)

Larry Munson followed Dick Shively as WSM sportscaster after working first at WKDA and then WSIX. He left the station in the mid-1960s to become an announcer first for the Atlanta Braves, then the Georgia Bulldogs. At WSM, in addition to his sports reporting, he also cohosted an afternoon radio program with Teddy Bart. Here former Vanderbilt and Chicago Bears quarterback Bill Wade (left) joins Munson (center) and University of Georgia sports information director Dan Magill (right) for a weekly football program spotlighting upcoming games. After his football career was over, Wade became an executive with Nashville's Third National Bank. (Grand Ole Opry archives.)

Eddie Hill was the longtime host of Channel 5's popular early morning *Country Junction* program. The show featured country music artists and bands and other live acts. Before joining WLAC-TV, Hill had hosted an all-night radio program on WSM radio. (Newschannel 5 Network, Nashville.)

Bob Lobertini was a very versatile member of the Channel 5 family. Although he was best known for being the station's longtime weatherman, he also hosted *Popeye* and *Slimnastics*, an exercise program. (Newschannel 5 Network, Nashville.)

When Larry Munson left the Atlanta Braves' announcing team after just one season, he returned to Nashville and joined WSIX-TV. Because of his popularity as one of the most highly recognized sports broadcasters in the Southeast, and because the station was still mired in third place in the ratings, Channel 8 decided to use Munson as the station's news anchor. The experiment did not work, and a year later, Munson went back to Atlanta, becoming the voice of the University of Georgia Bulldogs. (WKRN television.)

Many famous guests appeared with Jud Collins on the *Noon* show over the years. One of the loveliest was Hollywood actress Maureen O'Hara. WSM old-timers still talk about her visit to Channel 4 and the effect it had on the station's employees and *Noon* show crew. (Demetria Kalodimos.)

Barbara Moore was WSM's host for several entertainment and public affairs programs and frequently appeared on the *Noon* show. Prior to joining Channel 4, Craig Havighurst pointed out in his book *Air Castle of the South: WSM*, that Barbara had been an actress and foreign service official. (Demetria Kalodimos.)

Every weekday afternoon in the 1950s, WSIX-TV presented a movie and a feature called *Lucky Video*. Viewers sent in cards and letters, and each day, one was drawn by the program's host, Ken Bramming. If the viewer called the station within a certain amount of time, he or she won the cash jackpot, which often totaled several thousand dollars. (WKRN television.)

A Word on Words, featuring John Seigenthaler, editor of the Nashville *Tennessean* newspaper for many years, began on WDCN in 1972 and has been on the air now for more than 35 years. Each week Seigenthaler interviews an author about a book he or she has written. (WNPT television.)

Over the years, there have been a number of different combinations of WSM personalities on the nightly news. This trio in the late 1960s consisted of, from left to right, Dan Miller (news), Bob Olsen (weather), and Paul Eels, who had replaced Larry Munson (sports). (Demetria Kalodimos.)

Chris Clark spent 43 years at Channel 5, joining the station in 1966 as a reporter and news anchor. He retired from the station in 2007, having won an Emmy and a lifetime achievement award in broadcast journalism. (Newschannel 5 Network, Nashville.)

Channel Five is sporting a new face.

John Lashlee's face. He's Channel 5's new sportscaster. And he'll be seen Monday through Saturday at 6:20 p.m. and 10:20 p.m.

Lashlee's been around the sporting world for a long time. He began back in college by lettering in several major sports. In 1955, after serving four years during the Korean War and graduating from Broadcasting School, Lashlee became a sports announcer. He joined WLAC-Radio as sports director in 1962, and quickly became a favorite Nashville sportscaster and announcer.

In addition to his regular sports reports on WLAC-TV Lashlee will be the play by play announcer for Tennessee State University this fall.

Tune in Channel five and take a look at the face that goes along with a familiar voice. It won't be too long before John Lashlee is a familiar face too.

John Lashlee had done both news and sports at WLAC radio for a number of years in the 1960s before becoming its sports director in 1962. A few years later, he was moved over to the television side and became Channel 5's sports anchor. He also taught radio courses at the Midstate School of Broadcast Technique in Nashville, where one of his students was longtime Nashville radio newsman Buddy Sadler. (Metro Nashville Public Library.)

Hope Hines followed John Lashlee as the Channel 5 sports anchor, coming to the station in 1971. After four years, he left for a job in San Diego, but he returned to Nashville in 1983 and has been at WTVF (formerly WLAC) for the past 25 years, building a loyal following among Middle Tennessee sports viewers. (*Nashville!* magazine and the Metro Nashville Public Library.)

Bob Lobertini (right) joined Nashville exercise and fitness guru Jackie Bell (left) to cohost the weekday morning *Slimnastics* program on Channel 5 in the early 1960s. (Newschannel 5 Network, Nashville.)

Noel Ball, radio deejay and host of his own television show on WSIX, was often mobbed by teenaged admirers when they could get close to him. His star power was nearly as great as that of his famous guests like the Everly Brothers and Chase Webster (who wrote and recorded "Moody River"). (Vida Ball and WKRN.)

Bob Bell, in addition to anchoring the sports at Channel 8, hosted a midday program similar to Channel 4's *Noon* show. Here he interviews actor Chad Everett (far right), who in 1963 was starring as Deputy Del Stark on the television series *The Dakotas*. (Bob Bell and WKRN television.)

WDCN was Nashville's public television station, going on the air in September 1963 under the auspices of the Nashville–Davidson County Board of Education. Originally broadcasting on Channel 2 (in 1973, it swapped frequencies with WSIX), the station combined educational programs featuring metro-area teachers with network shows from National Public Television and other sources, such as National Geographic and public television stations in other cities. One of the more popular teachers in 1963 was Alice Kousser. (WNPT television.)

It was pointed out earlier that *Romper Room* on Channel 8 was hosted by three women over the course of its life in Nashville. When Miss Norma left the show in 1961, the second woman to host the program on WSIX was Eleanor Willis, or as the children knew her, "Miss Eleanor." (WKRN television.)

Miss Eleanor hosted the program for three years, leaving in 1964. The third and final host was Miss Nancy, whose name was not really Nancy but Beverly Early. Prior to her arrival, the program had decided to change all *Romper Room* hosts' names nationwide to "Miss Nancy." She continued with the program until it ended its run in 1973. (WKRN television.)

For 17 years, from the late 1950s throughout the 1960s, Dr. Ira North of the Madison Church of Christ was the quizmaster on a weekly religious program on WSIX-TV called *Know Your Bible*. The show also featured Charles Brewer and other local religious leaders, and was sponsored by Purity Dairies. (WKRN television.)

J. BILL FRAME
LEBANON DEMOCRAT

JULIE HOLLABAUGH
NASHVILLE TENNESSEAN

FRANK GLASS JR.
DAYTON HERALD

WSIX-TV had an early public affairs program, produced by the news department, which was like a local version of *Meet the Press*. Various elected and public officials were questioned by a panel of local news reporters like the three shown here. (WKRN television.)

WSIX, later known as WNGE and then WKRN, is still in the original building constructed for it on Murfreesboro Road more than 50 years ago. The local contractor hired to build the station was Pat Boone's father, Archie. (WKRN television.)

WSM, now known as WSMV, moved from its original location on Fifteenth Avenue South at Compton Avenue to its new home on Knob Road in 1966. The tower had already been there for nearly 10 years after being built to replace the one that collapsed in 1957. (Demetria Kalodimos.)

Channel 5 was proud of its sleek, modern, new studios on James Robertson Parkway when it moved there in 1968. Over the years, the facility has also served as the production headquarters for a number of network and syndicated programs, including *Hee Haw* with Roy Clark and Buck Owens. (*Nashville!* magazine and Metro Nashville Public Library.)

When it first went on the air in 1963, WDCN shared studio space with WSM-TV at Fifteenth and Compton Avenues. In 1976, it moved to its beautiful new home on Rains Avenue near the fairgrounds. (WNPT television.)

Eight

NASHVILLE TELEVISION GROWS UP

Nashville television during the past 25 years is vastly different from the first 25. Gone are the G-rated kids' programs with Westerns, cowboy heroes, and silly cartoons and puppets whose nose kids honked (Bobo the Clown) or rubbed (Poindexter the Dog). They have been replaced by superheroes and Power Rangers and lots of visual flash and audio noise patterned after the video games that spawned them.

College football and basketball games are still around, but now we also have soccer, volleyball, hockey, cycling, and X-games, with skateboards and scooters and bicycles that literally fly and then crash to the ground. Wrestling is still on television, but so is kickboxing, kung fu, karate, and the Ultimate Fighting Championship, where it appears anything is okay, and kicking, flicking, kneeing, and poking is legal. And speaking of poking, who ever thought people would sit in front of their televisions and watch people play poker?

As lifestyles have changed, broadcasting has, too. Radio stations now play every conceivable musical format, and instead of 8 or 10 stations in Nashville, there are more than 40. Instead of each station being owned by someone who started it or bought it for fun, those 40-plus stations are mostly owned by fewer than 10 different companies, all of whom are in it not for the love of broadcasting but for the love of money.

But with all of the changes in broadcasting, and many of them not for the better, one aspect has not changed, and for that many of us are grateful. The people in radio and television—both on-air talent and those behind the scenes—still do what they do out of love: love of the job, love of the station, and love for the listeners or viewers. As Teddy Bart so eloquently pointed out in his foreword to this book, they did what they did, and they do what they do, because there is nothing else they would rather do. And hopefully readers notice that every time they listen to their favorite radio station or watch their favorite television program.

Pat Sajak (left) and Dan Miller became good friends while working together at Channel 4. They later teamed up again on the West Coast when Pat hosted a late-night national television show and Dan was his announcer. (Dan Miller personal collection.)

Dan Miller joined WSM-TV in 1969. This is one of the earliest photographs of Dan at Channel 4, not at his familiar post behind the news desk but in front of the weather board. (Dan Miller personal collection.)

In this photograph are a mix of veteran broadcasters and newcomers. They are, from left to right, Boyce Hawkins (weather), Huell Howser (features), Dan Miller (news), Dave Daughtry (news), Bob Olsen (news), and Paul Eels (sports). (Demetria Kalodimos.)

Huell Howser is a native of Gallatin and a graduate of the University of Tennessee. After a brief stint on the staff of former Sen. Howard Baker, Huell was hired at WSM-TV to do human-interest stories. His *Happy Features* caught on quickly, and he became a viewer favorite. (Demetria Kalodimos.)

Many radio and television stations form basketball and softball teams to raise money for charity and gain goodwill and public relations among listeners and viewers. Channel 4's basketball team in the 1970s included, from left to right, (first row) Larry Garrison, Paul Eels, Aaron Mermelstein, Rudy Kalis, and Greg Powers; (second row) Larry Bearden, Dan Miller, Dave Daughtry, and manager Ralph Emery. (Demetria Kalodimos.)

Bill Hall & Snow Bird — 4 the Family

Bill Hall had been a newsman at WKDA radio before going to work for WSM. He took reporting the weather in Nashville to a new peak of popularity and is quick to give Snowbird part of the credit for his rise to fame. (Demetria Kalodimos.)

The men anchoring the nightly news at Channel 5 in the late 1960s and early 1970s made up one of the most popular news staffs at any Nashville station. They included, from left to right, John Lashlee (sports), Bob Lobertini (weather), and news coanchors Jerry Goad and Chris Clark. (Newschannel 5 Network, Nashville.)

Another longtime and very popular Channel 5 personality is Harry Chapman. Quite versatile, Harry has done the news, weather, sports, and even talk shows on the station. In this photograph, he is helping out on *Action Auction*. (WNPT television.)

Miller and Company was a longtime Channel 4 show hosted by Dan Miller with a different guest each week. Relaxing on the show's set are, from left to right, Dan, Charlie McAlexander, Lonnie Lardner, and Bill Hall. (Dan Miller personal collection.)

The cast continued to change at Channel 4 over the years. In 1976, viewers saw, from left to right, Carol Marin, who coanchored the news with Dan Miller, Paul Eels (sports), and Bill Hall (weather). (Demetria Kalodimos.)

The Channel 4 team in 1984 had changed again. Now it included, from left to right, Dan Miller (news), Demetria Kalodimos (news), Bill Hall (weather), and Charlie McAlexander (sports). Another person who was at WSMV about this time, but of whom there were no photographs available, was weatherman George Goldtrap. Viewers breathlessly watched as he flipped his chalk in the air, waiting to see if he would catch it in his lapel pocket or miss it. (Demetria Kalodimos.)

When Dan Miller left WSMV in 1986 to anchor the news at KCBS in Los Angeles, he was replaced by Jeff McAtee. Here is Jeff with the rest of the Channel 4 team. From left to right are Jeff, Demetria Kalodimos (news), Bill Hall (weather), and Rudy Kalis (sports). (Demetria Kalodimos.)

Bob Jordan has been a news reporter and anchor at WGN television in Chicago for many years, but he began his television career in 1970 at WSM as a booth announcer and news anchor for an early morning variety show. He left Nashville for the Windy City in 1973. (Bob Jordan and WGN television.)

Robin Roberts, for many years a reporter and sports anchor at ESPN, is now a cohost of ABC's *Good Morning, America.* Early in her career, she was a reporter at WSMV. This photograph shows Robin (left) and Demetria Kalodimos (right) helping out at an *Action Auction* on WDCN. (WNPT television.)

Sharon Puckett was a fixture at Channel 4 for 28 years, anchoring the news and specials features, before moving over to Channel 17. (*Nashville!* magazine and Metro Nashville Public Library.)

By 1981, Teddy Bart had left Channel 4 and was hired to anchor the news on Channel 2 with Anne Holt. The members of the news team were, left to right, Davis Nolan, Teddy, Tom Donovan, Anne, and Jim Bond. Despite the addition of Teddy and the growing popularity of Anne, the station still could not climb out of third place in the ratings. (WKRN television.)

John Seigenthaler Jr. joined the Channel 2 news team in 1992. After three years, he left Nashville to become a weekend news anchor on NBC and news anchor and program host on MSNBC. He now lives in New York and works for the family public relations firm Seigenthaler and Associates. (WKRN television.)

John Jr.'s father, now known as John Seigenthaler Sr., was still hosting his regular weekly program *A Word on Words* on WNPT-TV while his son was anchoring the news at WKRN. (WNPT television.)

Oprah Winfrey has become one of the most powerful and popular women in America, with her own television program, production company, and magazine. But after a brief period of reporting for WVOL radio as a teenager, she was an intern and then reporter for Channel 5, working with longtime news anchor Chris Clark. (Chris Clark personal collection.)

Stanley Siegel came to Nashville from Green Bay, Wisconsin. He hosted his own news and public affairs interview program on Channel 5, and during the short time he worked here, his abrupt style and abrasive personality created a lot of local controversy. He is shown here (center) in 1985. (*Nashville!* magazine and Metro Nashville Public Library.)

Creature Feature on Channel 4 was a popular weekly program on Saturday nights from 1971 until 1982. Its host was Sir Cecil Creape, played convincingly by WSM audio engineer and amateur actor Russ McKown. Pat Sajak honed his comedic skills recording voice tracks and cut-ins for this show and the *Sherlock Holmes* movies starring Basil Rathbone and Nigel Bruce on Channel 4's late-night programs. (Demetria Kalodimos.)

Public television's first big star was Mr. Rogers in 1968, followed by Big Bird on *Sesame Street* in 1969. From the late 1960s into the 1980s, a local WDCN personality, Miss Fran, kept kids entertained on *Jellybean Junction*, the *Music Fun Factory*, and *Mrs. Cabobble's Caboose*. Here she is in 1975 with the author's two daughters, Tracy (left), 9, and Eve (right), 4. (Author's personal collection.)

Nine

YESTERDAY AND TODAY

This trip down memory lane is nearly over. It began in 1922 with Nashville's first radio station and traveled well into the 1970s—more than half a century. As this book comes to a close, there is no better way to wrap it all up than to bring readers up to date on the people included on these pages. Some we know about, some we don't. If there is someone readers are interested in who is not on this page, feel free to e-mail the author [leeudorman@comcast.net], and he will find out what he can. For more information about the stations, the people, and the programs, check out www.NashvilleBroadcastingHistory.com.

Thanks for joining us today, and, as we always say on radio, "stay tuned, there's more to come."

Gone, but not forgotten: Jud Collins, Ott Devine, Grant Turner, Dave Overton, Boyce Hawkins, Bill Williams, T. Tommy, David Cobb, Ernie Keller, Ralph Christian, John McDonald, Paul Eels, Tom Tichenor, Jim "Ruffin Reddy" Sanders, John R., "Hoss" Allen, Herman Grizzard, Gene Nobles, Hugh Jarrett, Ken Bramming, Jim Kent, Buzz Benson, Bob Sticht, Noel Ball, Gene Clark, Audie Ashworth, Bill Berlin, Captain Midnight, DJ Dan Hoffman, Jack Sanders, Don Bowman, Bill Jay, Bob Lobertini, Gil Greene, Eddie Hill, Rick Moore, Barbara Moore, John Lashlee, Jack Stapp, and Dick Buckley.

Still around as of October 2008 but no longer on the air: Hairl Hensley, Bob Olsen, Tom Bryant, Ronn Terrell, Sam Hale, Larry Munson, Allen Dennis, Alan Nelson, Bill Hudson, Hudley Crockett, Khan (Charlie Brown) Hamon, Coyote McCloud, Rick Stuart, Frank Jolle, Gary Beaty, Mark Damon, Chris Clark, Bob Bell, George Goldtrap, John Seigenthaler Jr., Jerry Goad, Miss Norma, Miss Eleanor, and Miss Nancy.

Still active in broadcasting or a related field, here or somewhere else: Gerry House, Al Voecks, Mike Bohan, Duncan Stewart, Dave Nichols, Nick Archer, Chris Romer, Buddy Sadler, Hope Hines, Harry Chapman, Charlie Scott, Ted Johnson, Teddy Bart, Ralph Emery, Charlie Chase, Pat Sajak, J. Thomas, Huell Howser, John Seigenthaler Sr., Charlie McAlexander, Rudy Kalis, Jeff McAtee, Bob Jordan, Oprah Winfrey, Bill Hall, Lonnie Lardner, John Tesh, Van Irwin Jr., Scotty Brink, Bill Barry, and Bart Walker.

Teddy Bart's Roundtable was a fixture on Nashville radio for 21 years. It began on WLAC in 1984 with Teddy, Boyce Hawkins, Wayne Oldham, and John Bibb, then the sports editor of the Nashville *Tennessean*. In 1988, Karlen Evins joined the group, and in 1990, the program moved to WWTN-FM. In 1994, it shifted to WKDA when Teddy and Karlen bought that station, and then in 1999, it moved over to WAMB, where it remained until it finally went off the air in 2005. The cast of the *Roundtable* in this photograph includes the group as it was at the end of its two-decade run. From left to right are (first row) Teddy and Karlen; (second row) Adm. Jerry Breast, John Seigenthaler Sr., and Roy Neel. (Teddy Bart.)

The WSM radio and television family has always been a close-knit one. This reunion photograph includes, from left to right, Teddy Bart, Al Voecks, Jud Collins, and Dan Miller. Teddy came to Nashville in 1960 from Philadelphia and was singing and playing the piano in Printer's Alley when he was hired at WSM. In the 48-plus years that have followed, Teddy has hosted radio and television talk shows, created and hosted *Teddy Bart's Roundtable* and *Beyond Reason*, and written songs and several books. At WSM-TV, he was Jud Collins's successor as host of the *Noon* show. (Demetria Kalodimos.)

Oprah Winfrey grew up in Nashville and began her career here. Before working at Channel 5, she was a teenage reporter at radio station WVOL. At WTVF-TV, she began building her credentials and the winning style and personality that took her first to Chicago and then the country. (Metro Nashville archives, the *Tennessean*, and *Nashville!* magazine.)

Nashville's 'Heart and Soul' station reaches a milestone

by Norma White

When reaching this landmark it is usually referred to as the Big 40. So it is for WVOL.

For 40 years Nashville has had a voice over the airwaves entertaining listeners with music, news — good and bad, as well as having served as a training ground for some of the premiere talent in the entertainment industry.

Once known as WSOK-AM 1470, the station was the only voice committed to the African-American community for many years.

"WVOL has been the 'Heart and Soul' of the Nashville community and it has been the spokesperson to and for the community," stated station owner Sam Howard. "When we acquired the station, it was the mothership for WOOK."

Oprah Winfrey, at age 19, reads the news on the air at WVOL.

BIOGRAPHY

Combine a weatherman and a radio personality, throw in an occasional talk show host, and you've got PAT SAJAK.

Pat is WSM-TV's weekend SCENE AT SIX AND TEN weatherman and a WSM-AM Radio disc jockey from 3:00-5:00 Monday through Friday. Occasionally he replaces NOON SHOW host Teddy Bart, or weatherman Boyce Hawkins.

Pat came to WSM in 1972 after working at several radio stations in the South and Mid-West, including WNBS Radio in Murray, Kentucky and WEDC Radio in Chicago. He also served with the American Forces Radio Network while stationed in Saigon, Vietnam.

Born in Cleveland, Ohio and raised in Baltimore, Maryland, Pat graduated from Michigan State University in Lansing, Michigan with a Bachelor of Arts degree in journalism.

In a business where people are the greatest assets, WSM-TV and Radio truely have an asset in the vitality and sense of humor that are the trademark of Pat Sajak.

WSM·TV 4

Pat Sajak is fondly remembered by many Nashvillians who listened to him on WSM radio or watched him on Channel 4 in the 1970s. Obviously WSM believed they had discovered a real talent when they hired him for both radio and television. (Demetria Kalodimos.)

In 1999, Jud Collins (left), longtime news anchor and television host at both WSM and WSIX, reunited with old friend and former 1950s WKDA deejay Sam Hale (right). (Sam Hale.)

NINA LONG / STAFF

The queen bees of WKRN-Channel 2's *Romper Room* series of the 1950s and '60s returned to their old studio to reminisce last week as the station prepares for next year's 50th anniversary. The teachers of the lively little classroom are, from left, Eleanor Willis, Beverly Early and Norma Coverdale.

There were three women who hosted *Romper Room* on WSIX-TV over the years. They are seen here at a WSIX-TV reunion. From left to right are Eleanor Willis (Miss Eleanor), Beverly Early (Miss Nancy), and Norma Tate Coverdale (Miss Norma). (WKRN television.)

Didn't You Used To Be Bozo?

With his outrageous laugh, wild red wig and huge nose, Bozo the Clown dominated local kiddie shows for 25 years. Many people didn't realize that Bozo was a syndicated character — stations ordered his costume, and then hired their own talent. When WSM decided to start Nashville's first Bozo show in 1956, local puppeteer Tom Tichenor was cast as the first Bozo. "I was paid $5 for each live 15-minute show," he remembers. "I guess I became Bozo because I was handy. The make-up was awful, the costume too tight. There was never a script — it was just come in, put on the make-up, turn on the lights and you were on the air. It's amazing what you can do when you don't have any money and you have to fill time."

Tichenor left the show in 1959 to work with the Broadway production of *Carnival*. He remembers being "concerned that what I gave to children should have some class to it." Today, he's still entertaining children — with performances of his own marionettes at the Ben West Public Library. He confesses a preference for the kind of children's entertainment he's devised on his own. "I'm glad I didn't have to make a career out of Bozo," he says drily, "because a little Bozo goes a long way."

Tichenor was replaced by Dick Brackett, who had started out as a WSM prop man. "If the suit fits. . . ." Brackett quips about accepting the role. During his stint, the show changed from black and white to color, and moved to a larger studio to accommodate a bigger live audience of children. "It was live, spontaneous," he recalls. "Basically, we ad libbed the show

Bozo number three, Joe Holcombe

for nine years. If something went wrong, there would be a phone call. It seemed like Irving Waugh never slept — he watched every program that was on." Brackett often fell victim to children who told off-color jokes or uttered unprintable words — "No editing went out over the air," he stresses.

But unpredictable as they could be to work with, the children, Brackett believes, made the show work. "Kids were the stars of the show," he says. "The kids were so neat. They came with high expectations, and sometimes those expectations were met and sometimes they were disappointed." He wasn't sure how to answer when one little girl tugged at his arm during a show and asked, "Bozo, is there a man inside you?"

In 1966, WSIX decided Bozo was just the ticket to attract the after-school audience. In what was jokingly dubbed the "War of the Bozos" by the local press, they outbid WSM three to one for the rights to the show. Brackett, still with WSM, became Captain Countdown the Clown, and WSIX radio announcer Joe Holcombe won the role of Bozo after "several hundred people" auditioned. "I made it a game show," he explains. "We started the Bozo game show style right here in Nashville. The show went big-time, maybe 150 kids in the audience at a pop."

The format obviously worked — Bozo's show was number one in its time slot, and at one point kids in the audience were booked more than two years in advance. Holcombe enjoyed being Bozo. "I made him into a friendly bumpkin," he says, "the adult you could make fun of. He never did anything right." After Holcombe left the role, he remembers returning a year later to find his replacement "very nervous — he'd even smoke on the set in costume. It's not for everybody." But Holcombe always felt comfortable with the kids on the set. "I remember what it was like to be a kid," he says. "You can't learn that part."

Today Holcombe is back in radio announcing, hosting a morning program on WAMB. But occasionally, someone recognizes him and asks, "Didn't you used to be Bozo?" He generally replies, "I still am inside."

For, as he cautions, "There's a little Bozo in all of us."

Some say one should always leave the audience wanting more. Others say to always leave them laughing. What better way to do both than with the story of Nashville's version of a national television icon: Bozo the Clown. (*Nashville!* magazine and Metro Nashville Public Library.)

www.arcadiapublishing.com

Discover books about the town where you grew up, the cities where your friends and families live, the town where your parents met, or even that retirement spot you've been dreaming about. Our Web site provides history lovers with exclusive deals, advanced notification about new titles, e-mail alerts of author events, and much more.

Find Your Place in History.